OVERCOMING SHYNESS –
A WOMAN'S GUIDE

DIANNE DOUBTFIRE is a professional novelist. She has written novels for adults and teenagers, and two guides for writers. She also enjoys teaching creative writing. She lives with her husband in Hampshire.

Overcoming Common Problems Series

The ABC of Eating
Coping with anorexia, bulimia and
compulsive eating
JOY MELVILLE

An A–Z of Alternative Medicine
BRENT Q. HAFEN AND KATHRYN J.
FRANDSEN

Arthritis
Is your suffering really necessary?
DR WILLIAM FOX

Being the Boss
STEPHEN FITZSIMON

Birth Over Thirty
SHEILA KITZINGER

Body Language
How to read others' thoughts by their gestures
ALLAN PEASE

Calm Down
How to cope with frustration and anger
DR PAUL HAUCK

Comfort for Depression
JANET HORWOOD

Common Childhood Illnesses
DR PATRICIA GILBERT

Complete Public Speaker
GYLES BRANDRETH

Coping with Depression and Elation
DR PATRICK McKEON

Coping Successfully with Your Child's Asthma
DR PAUL CARSON

Coping Successfully with Your Child's Skin Problems
DR PAUL CARSON

Coping Successfully with Your Hyperactive Child
DR PAUL CARSON

Curing Arthritis Cookbook
MARGARET HILLS

Curing Arthritis – The Drug-free Way
MARGARET HILLS

Curing Coughs, Colds and Flu – the Drug-free Way
MARGARET Hills

Curing Illness – The Drug-free Way
MARGARET HILLS

Depression
DR PAUL HAUCK

Divorce and Separation
ANGELA WILLANS

The Epilepsy Handbook
SHELAGH McGOVERN

Everything You Need to Know about Adoption
MAGGIE JONES

Everything You Need to Know about Contact Lenses
DR ROBERT YOUNGSON

Everything You Need to Know about the Pill
WENDY COOPER AND TOM SMITH

Everything You Need to Know about Shingles
DR ROBERT YOUNGSON

Family First Aid and Emergency Handbook
DR ANDREW STANWAY

Feverfew
A traditional herbal remedy for migraine and
arthritis
DR STEWART JOHNSON

Fight Your Phobia and Win
DAVID LEWIS

Flying Without Fear
TESSA DUCKWORTH AND DAVID
MILLER

Overcoming Common Problems Series

Goodbye Backache
DR DAVID IMRIE WITH COLLEEN DIMSON

Good Publicity Guide
REGINALD PEPLOW

Helping Children Cope with Grief
ROSEMARY WELLS

How to Be Your Own Best Friend
DR PAUL HAUCK

How to Control your Drinking
DRS W. MILLER AND R. MUNOZ

How to Cope with Stress
DR PETER TYRER

How to Cope with your Child's Allergies
DR PAUL CARSON

How to Cope with your Nerves
DR TONY LAKE

How to Cope with Tinnitus and Hearing Loss
DR ROBERT YOUNGSON

How to Cure Your Ulcer
ANNE CHARLISH AND DR BRIAN GAZZARD

How to Do What You Want to Do
DR PAUL HAUCK

How to Enjoy Your Old Age
DR B. F. SKINNER AND M. E. VAUGHAN

How to Improve Your Confidence
DR KENNETH HAMBLY

How to Interview and Be Interviewed
MICHELE BROWN AND GYLES BRANDRETH

How to Love a Difficult Man
NANCY GOOD

How to Love and be Loved
DR PAUL HAUCK

How to Make Successful Decisions
ALISON HARDINGHAM

How to Pass Your Driving Test
DONALD RIDLAND

How to Say No to Alcohol
KEITH McNEILL

How to Sleep Better
DR PETER TYRER

How to Stand up for Yourself
DR PAUL HAUCK

How to Start a Conversation and Make Friends
DON GABOR

How to Stop Feeling Guilty
DR VERNON COLEMAN

How to Stop Smoking
GEORGE TARGET

How to Stop Taking Tranquillisers
DR PETER TYRER

If Your Child is Diabetic
JOANNE ELLIOTT

Jealousy
DR PAUL HAUCK

Learning to Live with Multiple Sclerosis
DR ROBERT POVEY, ROBIN DOWIE AND GILLIAN PRETT

Living Alone – A Womans Guide
LIZ MCNEILL TAYLOR

Living with Grief
DR TONY LAKE

Living Through Personal Crisis
ANN KAISER STEARNS

Living with High Blood Pressure
DR TOM SMITH

Overcoming Common Problems Series

Overcoming Common Problems

OVERCOMING SHYNESS –
A WOMAN'S GUIDE

Dianne Doubtfire

SHELDON PRESS
LONDON

First published in Great Britain in 1988 by
Sheldon Press, SPCK, Marylebone Road, London NW1 4DU

British Library Cataloguing in Publication Data

Doubtfire, Dianne
    Overcoming shyness: a woman's guide.—
    (Overcoming common problems).
    1. Women. Shyness
    I. Title II. Series
    152.4

    ISBN 0–85969–582–4

Photoset by Deltatype Ltd, Ellesmere Port, Cheshire
Printed in Great Britain by
Richard Clay Ltd, Bungay, Suffolk.

Life is not so complex if we do not so persistently make it so. We accept the results or the effects, but we concern ourselves all too little with the realm of cause. The springs of life are all from within.

RALPH WALDO TRINE

Contents

Acknowledgements

The author and publishers are grateful to the following authors
and publishers for permission to use copyright material:

Prentice-Hall, for excerpts from *Psycho-Cybernetics*, by Maxwell
Maltz.

Souvenir Press, for excerpts from *The Silva Mind Control
Method*, by José Silva and Philip Miele.

Unwin Hyman, for material from *Self Mastery Through
Conscious Auto-Suggestion*, by Emile Coué

Katharine Whitehorn, for an extract from a feature in the
Observer.

The author and publishers also acknowledge the use of quotations from James Alexander, Karen Blixen, James Hewitt,
Ralph Waldo Trine and *Vogue*.

The author would also like to extend warm personal thanks to
the following for their generous advice: Carol Barton, Sheila
Bishop, Dorothy Branco, Kathleen Clark, Margaret Thomson
Davis, Stanley Doubtfire, Vera Harvey, Tessa Krailing, Barbara
Lamb, Joy Peach, Sita Sheer, Marjorie Tepper, Mair Unsworth,
Constance White. And to Ena Richards, who not only suggested
improvements but also typed the final manuscript with great
speed and efficiency.

Introduction

No-one can expect to be confident all the time, but most of us could be a great deal more self-assured than we are. We need to understand the reasons for our shyness and then to persevere in a determined effort to overcome our inhibitions and develop the best that is in us. Without confidence we cannot function at peak efficiency, keep our bodies in good health, or cheer and encourage those around us. Confidence and happiness go hand in hand and I agree with Robert Louis Stevenson that 'There is no duty we so much underrate as the duty of being happy.'

The ability to cultivate self-assurance is of overwhelming importance, affecting everything we do, yet many shy people give no time to it, unable to accept the fact that their difficulties could be eased beyond measure by following a number of practical and well-tried principles.

There are no easy answers and I think it is useless, as well as unsympathetic, to suggest that people should 'pull their socks up' or 'snap out of it'. We need more constructive advice than that. I have discovered, through more than half a century of study and many failures, that there are laws at work in our lives which are as sure and infallible as the laws of mathematics. If we take heed of them, the results can be amazing; to ignore them is to starve in the midst of plenty. Yet many do ignore them, wasting their energies on regret and anxiety when these destructive and painful emotions could be greatly reduced.

If you are suffering from shyness, I think there will be something in the following pages to give you hope of a permanent cure. A deeper understanding of the causes of your problems and a fresh angle on how to overcome them could pave the way to an unexpected sense of security. So stay with me and let's explore the possibilities together. Wonderful changes can come about in a very short space of time.

Dianne Doubtfire 1988

1

What is Shyness?

Before we consider overcoming shyness, let's be sure that you really have a problem. Could it be that you are just delightfully gentle, modest, unassuming and self-contained? Many women are happy to remain on the side-lines, as it were, with no desire to take centre stage. You have only to visit a nursery school to realize that even very young children differ a great deal in temperament. There are the violets and the sunflowers and endless varieties in between; no book on shyness should try to change a woman's basic personality, only help her to express herself fully and creatively.

If you are content with your present role and find yourself in no way inhibited by self-consciousness, this book is not for you. Just relax in the knowledge that people who prefer to live quietly, doing what they feel is right for them, have just as important a place in the scheme of things as those who are more dominant.

If, however, you wish you could mingle and mix more freely, voicing your views, taking a firmer stand and working towards a stronger and more positive attitude, read on! Shy people miss out on so much in life and most of them could do a great deal to overcome the problem if they knew how to go about it. Some don't want to admit that they are shy, not even to themselves. Others pretend to be when they aren't, perhaps as an excuse for evading some activity they don't care for. It's important to be honest with ourselves about this, as about all things, but it isn't always easy; I sometimes find it harder to be honest with myself than with other people!

There are many degrees of shyness and many different aspects. Most people are shy on certain occasions and many are shy all the time. It's a kind of sickness and those who suffer from it would give anything for a magic potion which would cure them in one glorious gulp. 'She's painfully shy,' people say, but they probably have no idea just how painful it really is. Every outing

3

to a public place, every meeting with a stranger, every demand for self-assertion can be fraught with anxiety. I know all about it because I used to suffer myself.

There isn't a magic potion, of course, but there are many ways in which we can help ourselves to master the problem and sometimes they really do work like magic. I hope this book will set you well on the road to recovery.

I can only give you my own personal conclusions, born of a deep interest in the subject and a long experience of working with people who are shy, or who have managed to overcome their shyness to a very large extent. I understand how difficult it can be to triumph over such an ever-present and inhibiting situation and I hope you won't think I'm suggesting that the solution is a simple one. Nevertheless, a sincere desire to bring about a change and a determination not to be discouraged can work wonders, even for people who are very shy indeed.

Let's have a look at some of the definitions of shyness in the *Shorter Oxford Dictionary*: 'Easily frightened away; difficult of approach owing to timidity, caution or distrust; fearful of committing oneself to a particular course of action; chary, unwilling, reluctant; averse from admitting a principle or from considering a subject; cautiously reserved; wary in speech; shrinking from self-assertion; sensitively timid.'

Nervousness

Notice that the word 'nervous' never occurs. Shyness and nervousness are by no means the same thing, although a shy woman is perhaps more likely to suffer from nerves owing to her heightened sensitivity. Someone who is not shy may be afraid of thunder, mice or flying in an aeroplane, whereas a shy person may have no fear at all of these things. I can honestly say that I have now overcome my shyness to a very large extent, but I'm nervous of being trapped in a lift and I hate thunder. My husband is by nature reserved, but he has no fear at all of thunder or lifts.

Shyness is concerned with *other people*. We are not shy with a pet dog or cat, although we may be shy with children. We are not

4

shy when we are alone. I think we must accept the fact that we feel shy because we are anxious about other people's opinions of us. Shyness, therefore, seems to imply a sense of inferiority in some respect and the cure lies in overcoming this feeling and building up our self-esteem. It isn't easy, of course, but it can certainly be done and the rewards are quite amazing; a new life of confidence awaits you if you are prepared to make the effort. 'Making the effort' need not daunt you in the slightest. If you coax yourself along the right lines, gently but firmly, you will find the experience not only rewarding but enjoyable as well.

During the many interviews I have conducted with women who thought of themselves as shy, I have found that most of them admitted to a lack of self-esteem. But not all; some said they looked on themselves as somehow special, even superior, to their fellows and were shy because they didn't want to damage their image. I may be wrong, but I wouldn't call that shyness. I'd have thought that a person who is afraid of being given insufficient credit for her qualities or attainments must feel, to some extent, insecure. This kind of reticence seems more like vanity and could give the impression of unfriendliness.

It's very difficult to pin-point the various attitudes that lead to uneasiness in company but if we think honestly about our emotions, we shall be well on the way to feeling at home in the world. And isn't that what we all long for – to feel at home in the world?

Embarrassment

We have seen that nervousness is not the same thing as shyness, but what about embarrassment? This is closely connected with shyness and, in some cases, the two are almost indistinguishable. The main difference is that shyness is an ongoing condition whereas embarrassment hits us at certain times for specific reasons. We are embarrassed when we blush or stutter, and because embarrassment sometimes *makes* us blush or stutter, we can find ourselves in a vicious circle of distress – women who blush can be so much upset by it that they tend to avoid people altogether. We are embarrassed if we forget a person's name (especially if it's someone we have known for a long time!). It's partly because we don't want to hurt their feelings but possibly more because we think it makes us appear stupid; it often simply means we have other things on our minds and it's a perfectly normal occurrence for nearly everyone, young and old alike. There's no denying that we do seem to forget things more easily as we get older but we have only to think of those elderly actresses who remember their lines and cues, to be reassured that the ageing process doesn't *have* to impair one's memory.

However, let's get back to embarrassment. It's one of the most uncomfortable states we have to endure. It can happen quite unexpectedly and through no fault of our own, such as the day my small son went to answer the doorbell and shouted at the top of his voice: 'Mummy, there's a funny old tramp at the door!' It was an artist friend of mine – aged about thirty – who had come to tell me about a one-man show he was having at a local gallery. Luckily he had – and still has, no doubt – a good sense of humour. And oh, what an asset this can be when we are in an embarrassing predicament! If we can laugh at ourselves we have a great deal less to fear in this respect, but we wouldn't be human if these unfortunate happenings didn't make us go hot for a while. The secret of coping with them successfully lies in our own reaction. Honesty comes first. Never try to cover up; it always shows. If you forget somebody's name just be truthful and admit it: 'I'm so sorry but I can't think of your name – it's suddenly gone!' or something similar, according to the person and the situation. Far from feeling offended, many people are quite relieved to find that others are forgetful too. If they get uptight about it they probably have a personality problem of their own! So my advice is to be honest, never lose your sense of humour and put the incident out of your mind as soon as possible.

Famous people are often asked by television interviewers to tell us about their most embarrassing moments, which shows how entertaining these can be. I remember a glamorous young film star being asked this question and recounting how a vital piece of elastic broke when she was crossing the crowded entrance hall of a big hotel. Her frilly pink knickers fell round her ankles, making her stop in her tracks and drawing attention to her predicament. 'Whatever did you *do*?' she was asked. 'I just stepped out of them and put them in my handbag,' she said with a shrug. 'What else could I do?' Embarrassment, like shyness, only concerns our relationships with other people. We are not embarrassed watching a sexy television play alone, whereas we might be if a strait-laced friend were with us.

Nobody likes to appear foolish or ignorant, but we have to face the fact that none of us is perfect and we shouldn't worry about making mistakes from time to time. We must be tolerant not only of other people's errors but also of our own.

Self-consciousness

It seems to me that there is little or no difference between shyness and self-consciousness. In any case, they're both distressing! We may feel self-conscious even though we know we are being admired, either for our looks or for our accomplishments; the mere fact of being the centre of attention can cause a feeling of unease, due perhaps to the fear of failing to live up to expectations. Actresses tell me that they don't feel self-conscious on stage because (if they are acting well) they are safely concealed behind the character they are playing. Their main reasons for anxiety concern forgotten lines or missing props.

Analysing all the causes of shyness has made me understand, as never before, what a precarious life we all lead, and how delicate is the thread that separates calm self-assurance from pure panic! However experienced we may be in our various roles, we are prone to worry lest some unexpected development, some difficult person or our own inadequacy should spoil things for us. However, as I said earlier, everyone lacks confidence at some time or other. We can only do our best to strike a happy balance between undue reserve and overbearing bossiness.

Symptoms of Shyness

There are many ways in which your shyness can manifest itself. The most common, perhaps, is a difficulty in communication. The shy person (as I well remember from my own youthful experience) keeps herself to herself, avoiding conversation with strangers and only feeling comfortable with people she knows very well (and, even then, not all the time). One sometimes has the feeling that a shy woman is trying her best to be invisible! It's a question of being accepted. A well-loved friend or relation accepts us for what we are, with all our faults, whereas a stranger might not be so accommodating. Shy people are afraid of being criticized; they have a great many tender spots, feel vulnerable and are constantly worried about making mistakes or being rejected. To avoid the possibility of such humiliations (as they see it) they try to avoid saying or doing anything unless they are quite sure they can create a good impression.

I have a shy friend called Mary who is a truly brilliant tennis player. (All the names are fictitious, but my examples are based on true experiences.) Mary will gladly play tennis anywhere because she feels confident of her prowess. But in a café with friends after a match, she hardly says a word. She isn't very knowledgable or well educated and so she keeps out of any conversation that might betray her ignorance. If only she could be honest enough to admit her lack of knowledge, ask questions and listen with interest she would be a much more popular girl. She would also extend her horizons and consequently have less cause for shyness. People admire her skill at tennis, but they don't like her silence in the café because they see it as stand-offish and unfriendly. No-one minds if you don't know the answers, so long as you don't pretend that you do. In fact, we warm to people, don't we, when they make mistakes and forget things occasionally? If people are too perfect they point up our own shortcomings. Many women are shy because they expect too much of themselves. They want to appear faultless – in appearance, skill, knowledge, speech, etc. – and this kind of perfectionism can lead to unhappiness; nobody can live up to it.

Another symptom may be self-absorption. A shy woman is so

8

concerned with the impression she is creating that she finds it difficult to forget herself and show a genuine interest in other people. Yet that is one of the best ways of overcoming shyness and making friends. We all know people who ask us a question and then don't wait for an answer, but carry straight on about themselves. You have only to tell them you are going to France next year to spark off a story about *their* last visit to France, or the one they're planning. They won't ask you what part you are going to, or when, or how, or if you've been before. They aren't interested. This is often a symptom of shyness, because the self-absorbed person is afraid of other people and this fear has led to a kind of isolation which inhibits a cure. The answer is to make a real effort to ask people about their ideas and activities, to listen with attention and to resist the temptation to talk about yourself until you have given them a chance to respond. The people we like are those who care about our problems and don't talk more than half the time about themselves.

People who are too introspective can also lose that vital sense of wonderment at the world around them. Misery and suffering do abound but the marvels of nature are everywhere, and if we can rejoice in them while doing all that we reasonably can to alleviate the problems of others, we shall reach a higher level of confidence and contentment. Self-awareness has two sides: self-absorption is the negative side but a knowledge of our true place in the world is essential for our well-being.

Talking too much is often a cover-up for shyness. A person may be over-talkative in order to avoid a serious conversation which might betray some aspect of herself that she wishes to conceal. I know a Mrs M. who gabbles on incessantly; you can't get a word in edgeways. But I happen to know that her husband is serving a long prison sentence for armed robbery. This is one of those occasions when shyness and embarrassment overlap. She dreads any mention of her husband in case she might have to reveal the truth or to lie about him; therefore she talks incessantly on matters of her own choosing. Loyalty is preventing honesty. Both are fine qualities, but on this occasion it might be better if honesty were to triumph. If she could be honest about her predicament she would make sympathetic friends and feel a great deal more relaxed. We know there are some who would have no sympathy for her but in my view their friendship would hardly be worth having.

Some shy people gabble helplessly because they don't know how to stop. The solution here is to listen to the other person; you can't talk and listen at the same time!

If a relative behaves in ways that distress us and make us feel ashamed, it is usually best to be truthful about them if the matter arises in conversation. Many people have similar problems and we can find relief in sharing our feelings with others who understand. It will do us no good at all to suffer guilt on behalf of someone else, however close. I'm sure we can be happier and more at ease if we try to relate to other people with honesty, telling the truth, even if we feel it shows us up in a bad light. Confession *is* good for the soul and one confession often leads to another from the recipient, creating an atmosphere of mutual respect and sympathy.

Another symptom of shyness is continual defensiveness in the face of criticism. This may be due to a guilt complex which began in childhood, usually caused by a harsh or fault-finding parent. If you feel miserably put-down when someone points out a mistake, or constantly try to find excuses for every slip, why not make a real effort to accept people's comments with an easy grace, apologizing when necessary, explaining calmly if an explanation is called for, but never being over-sensitive to criticism?

If any of these examples prompt you to say to yourself: 'That's me!' then I hope you will find some helpful advice in the following pages.

2
Why are We Shy?
1. Problem Parents

When we understand the reasons for our shyness we are in a much better position to overcome it. You may already know the reasons for yours (I assume you are to some extent a shy person or you wouldn't be reading this book), but there may be other causes you haven't explored and I think it's important to face up to all the possibilities.

Parents are often to blame. Lack of love and caring, lack of understanding, too much criticism, neglect and sometimes violence – all can play their part in undermining a child's self-confidence and lead to a deep-seated shyness that persists into adult life even when the offending parent is no longer around. On the other hand, over-protection or over-indulgence can make a child unsure of herself. Grandparents may also have a lot to answer for on account of too much spoiling or too much carping. It isn't often that parents and grandparents all strike the right balance!

Mothers

For me, my mother was the culprit. She died in 1947, but I suffered for years from the insecurity her wounding words inflicted. Providentially, my father was strong and sympathetic. He did all he could to keep the peace, and his calm, philosophical approach to life helped me to bear my mother's unkindness. Without his influence I would probably not be in a position to write this book today.

You may be wondering what it was my mother said or did to upset me so much and I'll come to that later; none of her close relatives is alive so no-one will be hurt by my revelations. If you were fortunate enough to have a mother who was (or is) warm and understanding you may disapprove of the way I am speaking

11

of mine. 'Honour thy father and thy mother' is a precept many of us were taught at Sunday School and a great deal of guilt is engendered when our parents behave in such a way that we cannot honour them. But how can a child be expected to honour a father who gambles away his money, leaving his family penniless? Or an alcoholic mother who leaves young children alone in the house while she goes to the pub? Or any parent who is cruel, selfish or negligent? The subject may be painful to some of my readers but, if we are to get to the root of our shyness, we must be honest and fearless in our self-analysis; parents often damage their children's self-esteem and the reason they behave in this way is usually caused by their own personality problems, often dating back to *their* parents.

During my interviews on the causes of shyness I have come across a great many women who have been made to suffer deeply by their mothers. The cause is often jealousy on the part of the mother. Women may be jealous of their daughters for many reasons: the daughter's greater beauty or intelligence – or even merely for being young! But the most common reason, and by far the most dangerous, is the jealousy that results when a man loves his daughter, in whatever way and for whatever reasons, more deeply than he loves his wife. The subject may never be spoken of but all three are aware of it and, in many cases, the wife will turn against her daughter on this account, putting her down in all manner of ways, subtle or not so subtle. The child, who naturally longs for the love and support of both her parents, is driven to dislike her mother. This exacerbates the problem, making the mother more aggressive, and an increasingly unhappy family situation is bound to develop. The daughter becomes either withdrawn or rebellious, depending on her nature but, which-ever way it goes, she may find herself lacking in self-assurance as a result.

Jealousy may also result when a girl is offered greater opportunities than her mother ever had. The mother is tied to the house, perhaps with other children to look after, and the daughter goes off to university or lands an interesting job, wears dashing clothes, has holidays abroad and probably marries some gorgeous man who (understandably perhaps) isn't all that fond of his mother-in-law. The daughter, although she may seem to have everything going for her, is suffering from resentment and a sense of insecurity as a result of her mother's antagonism. (We'll come to fathers later!) If, on the other hand, the daughter fails to achieve her ambitions, that, of course, is another reason for shyness – a sense of inferiority.

Parents sometimes have very high expectations for their offspring, so high or unsuitable that they cannot be fulfilled. Low expectations are also a problem ('*She'll* never pass those exams!'). In either case the girl may feel worthless and lose interest in any kind of satisfying work.

I knew a young wife called Jennifer who used to be extremely shy. 'I can't *do* anything,' she'd say. 'I'm hopeless at everything I try.' Her mother had a bright, outgoing personality and was an excellent cook and hostess, with many admiring friends. Jennifer had always been overshadowed and although her mother wasn't actively unkind, she was always telling her daughter to 'get going' and 'make an effort' until the poor girl grew so dissatisfied with herself that she gave up hope and withdrew into lethargy. When she met a charming man in her office who actually wanted to marry her, she couldn't believe she deserved him and was jealous of every attractive girl he talked to.

Everything changed when she married him and learned to cook. He bought her Delia Smith's *Complete Cookery Course* and encouraged her to try the recipes. He was so appreciative of her efforts that she joined a cookery class at the local Adult Education Institute. She made new friends, overcame her shyness to a very great extent and now gives dinner parties for six without a qualm. Her mother has a new respect for her although, of course, she has to find fault with some detail ('Haven't you put a weeny bit too much salt in the sauce, dear?'). But Jennifer has gained self-confidence, thanks to her husband's encouragement and to her own efforts. If you feel a lack of achievement, your own shyness might well disappear in a similar way (see *Discovering hidden talents* on page 44).

The mother who is over-protective and over-anxious can also

deprive her daughter of self-confidence. 'Be careful – you'll drop it and stain the carpet' when a little girl wants to carry a cup of tea across the room is the kind of attitude that leads to shyness. When we are trusted to do things well, we are much more likely to succeed. The child who is continually being warned against hurting herself, catching cold, losing her purse (or being mugged or raped) is very likely to grow up timid and apprehensive. Obviously we must understand the dangers and take no needless risks, but the girl who is forbidden to wear make-up, visit discos, invite her boyfriend home or go camping is probably the one who has received no accurate sex information from her mother and who is therefore more vulnerable on account of her naïvety. The narrow-minded or over-anxious mother, whose intentions are worthy but misguided, is often the cause of her daughter's shyness. Anyone who takes away our initiative reduces our self-confidence. Equally damaging is the 'don't speak until you are spoken to' attitude, which builds up the kind of inhibitions that can last a lifetime if nothing is done to eradicate them.

If any parent, however amenable, expects a daughter to live at home, giving up her own freedom (including perhaps the chance of marriage) there is bound to be a problem unless the daughter has no wish to do anything else with her life. Women who have accepted such a role, either willingly or unwillingly, are often very shy.

As for my own experience, when I was six my mother cut the head off my teddy-bear as a punishment for some childish misdemeanour. When I was sixteen she said no man would ever love me. On my wedding day she told me I looked 'hideous' (I was wearing lipstick and she disapproved of make-up!). Those three examples are enough to explain my own predicament and I know that many of my readers will have suffered in similar ways. Jealousy of my father's devotion to me was, I now realize, the reason for her continual vindictiveness but a jealous nature may in itself be the result of insecurity brought about by a difficult parent. The chain must be broken and, whatever the reasons for your own childhood suffering, *you* are the one to break it. You do not have to allow an unsympathetic or misguided parent to influence you for ever. You must take immediate action to free yourself. It *can* be done. I did it myself.

Fathers

Let's face up, first of all, to the tragic problem of sexual assault. We cannot overlook this deeply disturbing aspect of parental damage; no girl can be expected to remain unscathed by such a trauma and the resulting neurosis may need professional treatment. Rape by anyone is bound to have a serious psychological effect but any kind of sexual interference by a father or stepfather may result in a type of extreme reserve that is outside the scope of this book. If you are unfortunate enough to be suffering in such a way, you should consult your doctor who will arrange for appropriate therapy. Alternatively, contact one of the addresses given in the Appendix.

Ill-treatment of any kind by a girl's father can make her shy but it can also make her suspicious of all men, unless she guards against it. She must convince herself that many men – most men, in fact – are kindly and supportive. This doesn't mean that, in spite of this, they can't be thoughtless and selfish, but doesn't this apply to women as well? We all have our faults; a great deal of tolerance is required on both sides for a happy relationship. I won't say 'marriage' because there are many happy couples living together outside marriage (and many unhappy ones inside it). The important thing is for a man and a woman to love and respect one another, giving and taking equally. A difficult father or mother can cause great misery but the past is behind you and you can, with courage and determination, minimize the pain and look forward to a confident and stable future.

If you have a difficult parent who is still around, making your life unbearable, then I think you should consider getting away. Nobody has the right to destroy another person's peace of mind. However, even if you are not living under the same roof, there may be visits, letters or phone calls, which can have a damaging effect unless you develop a strong inner resistance to those all-too-familiar jibes and innuendoes. Tell yourself that you don't

15

have to be upset; it's really up to you. We all have far more control over our emotional reactions than we may imagine.

We cannot avoid realities, and some women are unavoidably burdened with the care of such a parent (or grandparent). In these cases the best compromise is to develop outside activities and friendships, adopting as calm and kindly an attitude as possible to the problems at home. It isn't easy, but nervous tension is bad for all of us and it can usually be reduced if we make a concerted effort along the right lines, using current techniques of relaxation and thought control. The late Dr Maxwell Maltz, M.D., F.I.C.S., a well-known psychologist and plastic surgeon, stated that just as our body maintains a temperature of 98.6 degrees Fahrenheit, regardless of the climate, we also have a built-in 'spiritual thermostat' that enables us to maintain a steady emotional temperature, despite the atmosphere around us. He wrote in his book *Psycho-Cybernetics*,

> Many people do not use this spiritual thermostat because they do not know it is there; they do not know that such a thing is possible, and they do not understand that they do *not have* to take on the outward climate. Yet your spiritual thermostat is just as necessary for emotional health and well-being as your physical thermostat is for physical health.

These facts are of vital importance when we consider mastery over shyness. Later I shall discuss them in detail.

Parents who are constantly quarrelling can disturb a child's peace of mind and make her wary. Her natural desire for a good relationship is undermined and she may find men intimidating. Another factor is the deprivation she must feel at being denied the happy family atmosphere she finds in other girls' homes. Having parents who are divorced or separated can also destroy self-confidence, especially if the parent she lives with forms a new partnership with someone the daughter finds unsympathetic.

Being illegitimate or adopted is sometimes a reason for self-consciousness, though it really shouldn't be. As always, we must surely concentrate on being the best person we can, here and now, with no useless worries about the past.

Finally, if it's at all possible, talk to a difficult parent about his or her childhood. Terrible things may have happened that will make you understand their behaviour – if they are able to communicate with you honestly. Fear, insecurity, sexual hang-ups or nervous disorders may cause a parent to behave unjustly. Some of us, as parents ourselves, know this to be true. I hope I was a sensible and understanding mother but I know I behaved badly to my son – and to my husband – when I was suffering from pre-menstrual tension. At last I found the courage to talk about it openly with the two of them; I felt a lot better about it – and so did they.

There are endless reasons for shyness connected with parents. Later I shall analyse the ways in which, according to your own particular personality, you can come to grips with the problem, feel more confident and enjoy a much more carefree and creative life.

3

Why are We Shy?
2. Other People

A friend of mine once said, 'I'm sure I could be perfectly happy if it weren't for other people!' We all feel like that sometimes. Other people certainly have a great deal to do with our shyness.

Siblings

I'm an only child myself but I have heard many first-hand dramas of the suffering caused by brothers and sisters and the consequent lack of self-assurance. Teasing – although it may seem a minor problem to those who have never been tormented by it – can do a great deal of damage to a sensitive youngster.

Let's consider first the situation of the only child. I've never really regretted being the only one; it gave me a sense of independence that I treasure. Another bonus was reading. We lived in the country and, feeling lonely, I was introduced to the joy of books at an early age by my father. Of course, there are disadvantages; reared in a kind of isolation, the only child may find it difficult to relate to other children and the attention and over-indulgence she often receives at home can make her self-conscious and over-sensitive. Siblings are bound to 'knock the corners off' and provide companionship, enabling a girl to cope more easily with school life.

A girl called Sophie, however, was subjected to such persistent harassment by an elder brother that she ran away from home at the age of eleven and lived with an aunt for several years. Now, in her twenties, she is so painfully withdrawn that she finds it almost impossible to enter into conversation with a stranger. Her aunt explained to me that Sophie's brother, five years older, could not bear to forfeit the sole attention of his parents and consequently plagued his baby sister right from the start. It's a textbook situation, of course, but none the less painful. 'He made me

18

frightened of everybody,' Sophie told me. I asked her if she could talk to him about it, now that they are adults. She gave a dry laugh. 'He's never listened to anything I say and he certainly isn't going to start now. Anyway, I never see him if I can help it.'

Fortunately most brothers are supportive, helping their sisters to cope with problems, introducing them to their friends, building confidence rather than taking it away. Many sisters, too, enjoy a wonderfully close and happy relationship with one another but there could be many reasons for resentment to develop. An elder sister may be jealous of a new arrival. A girl with a sister who is prettier, more accomplished or who appears to be more in favour with the parents is bound to feel a sense of inferiority, which can lead to shyness. Later there may be rivalry over boyfriends.

Enid is an elderly friend of mine who always struck me as being very timid. When I began this book I asked her if she felt she was shy and, if so, could she identify the cause. Yes, she had always suffered from acute shyness, she said. And then she hesitated. 'No, not always,' she went on. 'Something happened when I was five which took away my confidence and I never seem to have got it back. My sister is three years older than I am and she was playing with another little girl of about eight when I asked to join them in a game. "No!", said my sister but I pleaded and stayed. After a while my sister said to her friend, "Never mind, let's just pretend she isn't there!"' From that day forward, Enid suffered from a terrible lack of self-esteem. It was, of course, a lack of *identity*. A feeling of one's own individuality, one's own unique place in the world, is essential for happiness; Enid's sister, in her eight-year-old ignorance, destroyed Enid's self-assurance on one never-to-be-forgotten day. 'I can never understand how anyone can *like* me,' she said. I was astonished. She is a kind and warm-hearted lady, delightful in every way, and I told her so.

She is now an elderly widow. What could she have done about her problem if she had thought about it sooner? Would it ever have been possible to overcome such a deep-seated sense of her own worthlessness? Yes, of course it would. And if you are in a similar position, I think you will find some practical advice in the following pages.

19

Teachers

An unsympathetic teacher can do lasting damage to a child's self-esteem. When I was at school we had a maths mistress who seemed to enjoy humiliating those of us who were slow at arithmetic. I can still remember the panic I felt when she called me out to the front and made me do a sum on the blackboard, encouraging the class to laugh at my mistakes.

One of my friends had a similar problem with sport. She just wasn't built for gymnastics and went through agonies of dread when she was faced with the vaulting horse. Luckily we had a sympathetic gym mistress who never said anything to embarrass her.

Teachers who ridicule their pupils have a lot to answer for. Often their own insecurity is the problem; they know they can get a cheap laugh at the expense of an anxious child. If your shyness has been brought about by this kind of treatment, it's a comfort to remind yourself that you are no longer a girl in class at the mercy of a thoughtless or sadistic teacher but a sensible, independent adult, free at last from such strictures. We don't have to suffer for ever because we were put down as children. As soon as we accept this fact (and it *is* a fact) we are on the way to that self-confidence which is our birthright.

It simply isn't true that we can be conditioned for life by the time we are seven, and Freud has caused a great deal of hopelessness and despair by expounding this theory. The latest scientific findings tell us that the engrams of the brain, which record childhood traumas and were thought to be permanent, can in fact be changed for the better by our present mental habits. Dr John C. Eccles, an expert in the field of brain physiology, says that when we experience something, an amazingly complex pattern of neurons is set up in the brain tissue. These patterns, or 'engrams', are stored away for future use and are reactivated whenever we recall a past experience. When we think, remember or imagine, these neurons discharge an electric current that can be measured, and each time they are played back, says Dr Eccles, these neural engrams take on some

20

of the tone and temper of our present mood. The choice is up to us as to which we select for 'playback'. In his invaluable book *Psycho-Cybernetics*, Dr Maltz tells us that:

> This gives us reason to believe that unhappy childhood experiences are not as permanent as some earlier psychologists would have us believe. We now know that not only does the past influence the present, but that the present clearly influences the past. In other words, we are not doomed or damned by the past. Because we did have unhappy childhood experiences which left engrams behind, does not mean that we are at the mercy of these engrams. . . . Our *present thinking*, our *present mental habits*, our attitude towards past experiences, and our attitudes towards the future – all have influence upon old recorded engrams. The old can be changed, modified, replaced by our present thinking.

History abounds with examples of courageous men and women who have risen above the painful influences of their early days. In many cases they have learnt and profited by the misery they suffered, helping others to overcome similar problems.

So, if your confidence was taken away from you in childhood, you must fight to reclaim it. 'Fight?' you may say, 'but I'm not the fighting kind!' Maybe not, but surely a positive struggle for strength and balance and serenity is right and necessary for all of us? We say that 'God helps those who help themselves', and when I meet a woman who has been crushed in early life by an unsympathetic relative or teacher, I always encourage her to work very hard to rise above those negative influences.

The next big problem is the whittling away of self-esteem by a husband or lover who is wielding his influence here and now. Not so easy to combat as having been put down in childhood, but the difficulty must be faced and there are many ways in which a woman in this predicament can establish a position of greater strength and independence.

Husbands and lovers

A loving and understanding husband or lover can build up a shy woman's self-esteem and restore the confidence her parents or teachers may have undermined. On the other hand, a selfish and domineering man can destroy a woman's sense of her own identity, however well-adjusted she may have been before she met him. (I shall use the words 'husband' and 'wife' to include couples who form long-term relationships outside marriage.)

We have all come across the kind of man who belittles his wife in company and will not allow her the freedom to be her own person. This is often based on a deep sense of insecurity on the part of the husband; he can't bear the thought of 'the little woman' venturing into so-called male territory and making a success of it. He may want to keep her in the traditional role of cook–housekeeper so that she will always be there to serve him. He may try to suppress her talents (I know women whose husbands have torn up their writing and burnt their paintings). If she finds the courage to go against his wishes he will make her suffer for it; he may keep her short of money or try to break her spirit with moodiness or even violence.

Some of my readers will know exactly what I'm talking about. Those who don't should thank their lucky stars! Many women have poured out their hearts to me and I know that there are few problems more difficult to cope with than a partner who is bent on causing friction if his wife wishes to preserve her independence. She feels as if her very identity is being eroded.

What, then, is the best course of action? If she loves him and wants to continue the relationship, she will need to build up an inner defence against his hurtfulness, breathing the clean air of detachment and becoming involved in as many rewarding projects as possible. I can imagine some of my readers, oppressed by a difficult man, thinking: 'Develop a sense of detachment? She must be joking!' But I'm not joking, as you will see in Chapter 10 on Relaxation. If you are prepared to work at it, you will find amazing benefits through the power of the mind. You will be able to distance yourself from many of the painful experiences that come your way and find your own still centre of peace despite the turmoil around you.

If this is a problem in your life, do all you can to make him understand your feelings. Communication is essential for any good relationship. It may be that he simply does not realize how much damage he is doing; a heart-to-heart talk nearly always brings about a better rapport. He, too, may have anxieties he needs to tell you about but hasn't felt able to discuss.

Another problem is the flirtatious husband who not only makes his wife feel jealous but induces a sense of failure. Some men need admiration to bolster their own insecurity, especially as they get older (and so do women, of course!), so we mustn't take it too seriously. 'Ignore it' is the best advice, I think, but a man who constantly remarks on the beauty of other women, drawing attention to his wife's shortcomings, can be a real reason for lack of self-esteem and consequent shyness.

An unfaithful, harshly critical or violent husband is such a threat to a woman's health and happiness that she may be wise to take the matter to a counsellor at Relate (see Appendix). Separation could be the only course and, although it may seem impossibly difficult with regard to finance, especially if she has a young family, a break might be better in the long run both for her and for the children. We have seen how a domineering or uncaring father can destroy a child's confidence and I have always thought it was misguided to perpetuate an unhappy marriage 'for the sake of the children'. Men who make us afraid of them reduce our sense of security and freedom, both of which are essential for our emotional well-being.

You might think it irresponsible of me to advise any woman to leave her husband but I know many a browbeaten wife who stays on, year after year, not only resentful and unhappy but often suffering a nervous breakdown or other illness as a result. I also know women who have made the break, in spite of the problems involved, and who are now living full and useful lives.

A friend of mine left her husband some years ago because he allowed her no freedom or money and was constantly finding fault with her, although she did everything she could to please him. She has found a satisfying job as housekeeper to a disabled old lady and it's a joy for me to see her so well and happy. Her teenage children, free at last from the constant friction with their father, are sure she has made the right decision both for them and for herself.

I have another friend whose husband used to bolt the door against her at night if she went to an Italian class in the local town. 'Why the hell does she want to learn Italian?' he fumed when I told him what I thought of him. 'She'll never go to Italy – not if I can help it!' Luckily she had the pluck to stand out against him and she stayed the night with me after her classes. Now she is divorced and her new man took her to Rome for their honeymoon. Some true stories *do* have happy endings!

A very different situation sometimes arises when a woman has such a close relationship with her husband that all other friendships are excluded. She may feel ill at ease with anyone else, thinking that no-one but he could possibly understand her; she feels threatened by the big world beyond their cosy twosome. I think it is unwise to cut oneself off in this way from so many rewarding people and activities, not only because it creates such a narrow existence but also because she will suffer an even greater depth of loneliness than need be if she should lose him. It is a great mistake to become too dependent on any one person, even in a happy marriage, but women who lack confidence have a tendency to cling and to avoid new commitments. If this is your problem, why not join a class or group, take a short holiday without your husband or simply have lunch with a friend once a week? You'll find that occasional activities apart will enhance your relationship.

Colleagues at work

When we finish our full-time education we may, if we are shy, feel anxious about our future in employment. A new job can seem very daunting, but in many cases the day-to-day contacts with other adults in the same environment gradually make us feel more at ease.

24

Sometimes, however, we may come up against an overbearing character who will undermine our confidence unless we guard against it. There are the know-alls who will tend to make us unsure of ourselves when we are learning new ways and techniques. Or a man in the same office will make passes at us and won't take no for an answer. The boss could be intimidating. Someone with a power complex might show off at the expense of a newcomer. And, of course, there will be those who tease us and play pranks on us.

Few women escape some kind of conflict in a new place of work; the very fact that she is inexperienced and eager to succeed can cause problems for a woman who is inclined to underrate herself. As always, a sense of humour is vital, together with a determination not to be touchy or shockable (there's bound to be a certain amount of vulgarity around!) and to be honest about our difficulties, never pretending that we understand the work when we don't. Above all, in difficult situations take a deep breath, relax your shoulders and resolve to let nothing get you down. It's a great morale booster if you can prove to yourself that you are able to keep cool when many wouldn't.

4

Further Reasons for Shyness

Health

How can a woman be self-confident, you may ask, if she has been condemned to take a back seat in life owing to poor health or disablement? Enforced exile from the ordinary world over a lengthy period can produce feelings of isolation and inferiority unless the sufferer is a person of great courage and character. (Nervous disorders may give rise to shyness, but this is a separate problem and requires specialist treatment.)

The wisest course is to keep abreast of the times by reading widely, listening to the radio, cultivating a number of good friends and avoiding self-pity. If you are cheerful and don't talk too much about your ailments, people will be happy to visit you. If you moan, you will scare them away, and they will only come to see you as a duty and not because they enjoy your company. A positive attitude and a caring interest in others are the key qualities to bear in mind if you are losing confidence on account of poor health. Aren't they, in fact, the key qualities for everyone, in every situation?

I had a friend called Geoffrey Smith who was not only blind but confined to a wheelchair with multiple sclerosis. He heard on local radio that I was a tutor in creative writing and phoned to ask if I could give him some lessons as I lived nearby. Needless to say, I agreed, but I couldn't have guessed what pleasure and inspiration I should find in his friendship. I visited him regularly for nearly ten years until he died in 1984 and I used to look forward very much to those visits. He even used to cheer me up if I was feeling low! He was full of new ideas, never complained and always wanted to hear about my own activities. We laughed a lot and he was extremely hard-working in learning the craft of writing. He used to battle against enormous difficulties, recording his articles on to one tape-recorder and correcting them on another, never failing to revise because it was too much trouble. As a result, he had many articles published in leading periodicals. His first success was a light-hearted piece in *The Guardian*, giving advice to sighted people on how they should treat the blind.

Here is an extract from the last article he wrote, shortly before his death.

In disablement, thoughts are of paramount importance; they can lead a person either down a lonely road to misery or to new and refreshing pastures. The choice lies with each individual. In my view, there's no point in sitting around asking 'Why me?'. It's a question to which I believe there's no answer. I also try to avoid looking inwards at my own problems; it only makes me self-centred, miserable and boring company.

How did he manage, you may ask, to think so positively? He did it through relaxation and meditation, and I hope you will be able to develop similar powers, no matter what your problem may be.

Anyone in poor health should try to become involved in some kind of serious study. Before he began writing, Geoffrey used to feel as if he were 'on the scrap heap', as he called it. You may think he was lucky to have the talent and, of course, that's true, but I think we all have some kind of talent if we seek it out and develop it (see page 44).

Homosexuality

Lesbians have always been forced by society to feel reticent or even ashamed. Unless they have the courage to 'come out', they dread their secret being discovered, and the constant living of a lie is bound to undermine self-confidence. A woman's sexual tendency is her own concern and, in my opinion, no-one should make her feel guilty or embarrassed about it. I recently went on holiday with a woman friend and one day, as we came out of our hotel room, she whispered to me, 'Wouldn't it be awful if people thought we were lesbians!' We are both married and it didn't seem likely in any case, but I thought how sad it must be for women who are homosexual to be faced with this kind of attitude. Some are even rejected by their parents.

Many lesbians must have a shyness problem. The media create prejudice and it can't be easy to belong to a minority which attracts so much critical attention. Clause 28 won't help, but I suppose the best solution is to be open about it. 'To thine own self be true. . .'.

Class

The divisive British class system causes a lot of shyness. (And so, of course, does our natural British reserve!) It isn't easy for a working-class girl to feel relaxed at dinner in a smart restaurant with an upper-crust boyfriend. It's not just a matter of knowing which knives and forks to use; there's the problem of coping with all manner of unexpected occurrences that might betray her. Sadly, we have all been conditioned to think of the working class as inferior, and those who aren't well versed in upper-class behaviour may be secretly ashamed of it. So what is the solution? Honesty, of course. It's so much easier if we admit our ignorance and ask for information.

Education, having so much to do with opportunity, is closely connected with class. A woman without academic qualifications may understandably feel shy in the company of a university graduate, but remember that a great many successful people had little formal education. If you have a problem here, lack of schooling can usually be rectified by adult education courses.

The class system, however, can be a veritable hot-bed of misery for those with humble beginnings, as I know to my cost. A regional accent can be an embarrassment if you let it be, but it's far better to speak normally than to adopt a phoney 'educated' way of speaking. These days it really does not matter. Think of all the famous and distinguished people who are proud of their natural dialect and make no effort to change.

I spoke broad Yorkshire as a child and, when I went to stay

28

with relatives in the south, I felt ill at ease because my cousins used to mimic my accent. They were only teasing but it made me unwilling to talk. When I moved to London at the age of twenty, I gradually picked up the 'King's English', as it was called in those days, although even now I sometimes burst out with broad vowels when I'm excited. You might consider taking elocution lessons if your native accent really bothers you.

The main thing to do if you are shy of venturing into areas outside your original beginnings, whether higher or lower, is to tell yourself that it simply *does not matter*, and those who think it does should be disregarded. It's the person you are that matters, not how you speak or how familiar you are with formal etiquette. Good manners don't belong to any particular class; they belong to a natural consideration for other people's happiness and comfort.

Clothes

It's no use denying that clothes are very important indeed to the average woman. If we don't feel at ease in what we are wearing we can't expect to be relaxed. My parents couldn't afford to buy me the regulation school gymslip and my mother made one for me that was a slightly different colour and style. I went through agonies over that gymslip! Children hate to be different.

As adults we should wear the clothes we feel happy in. They don't have to be new or smart, but they should express our personality. When I said this to a very shy friend she laughed and told me that if she did, she'd never wear anything but grey so she could fade into the background! She did, in fact, wear a lot of grey and brown, but I suggested that she liven it up with splashes of red or yellow to express the sparkle of humour behind her reticence. She took my advice, and recently she actually bought a red coat and looks stunning in it. Bright colours are cheering to wear and also a pleasure to those around us; if you feel your clothes are on the drab side, why not lash out on something a little more daring?

Here is some good advice I read long ago in a woman's

magazine: next time you have a couple of hours to spare, go through your wardrobe and sort out all the clothes that do nothing for you. Try them on to see if there's scope for alteration or new accessories; if not, give them to a jumble sale or sell them to a Nearly New shop. It's much more satisfying to have a small collection of clothes you really love than a large wardrobe bulging with items you would rather never wear again. I haven't followed this advice myself for years and when I've finished writing this book I shall spend an afternoon on it. But I won't part with any clothes that I love but can't get into; they are a splendid incentive for losing weight – and losing weight would be very good for my own self-esteem!

Money and taste have a lot to do with the way we dress. For those who are young and good-looking, the problem need hardly arise; a pretty woman under thirty looks gorgeous in almost anything (although she seldom believes it). When we are older, however, or not particularly handsome, clothes can present a daunting challenge, especially for those of us who have to dress on a modest budget. Changing fashions and rising prices can cause great distress to women of all ages. If you can sew it's not so bad but if, like me, you have to rely on ready-to-wear clothes to flatter a less-than-perfect figure, you must use whatever flair for style and colour you can muster to keep yourself looking good and so maintain your self-assurance.

Hair and make-up are important, too, to most of us. When I come out of the hairdresser's I feel a great deal more confident than when I went in! But however immaculate our appearance may be, the real source of confidence lies deep within ourselves, a sense of our own true place in the scheme of things. This has nothing whatever to do with a shabby coat, scuffed shoes or untidy hair.

Money

Shortage of money, as most of us know from experience, is often the cause of embarrassment. If the shortage is prolonged for months or years, it can also become a reason for shyness. We may become timid and cautious in our relationships purely because we can't afford to share expenses, pay for meals out or entertain friends in our homes. Children who are given less pocket money than their classmates may become shy as a result, opting out of friendly gatherings in case their penury is exposed.

If we don't have the right dress for a certain occasion and can't afford to go out and buy one, we tend to find some excuse to refuse the invitation. If our rooms are small and shabby, we may not like to invite other people there unless we are sure they won't feel critical. And isn't that the secret? Shortage of money is a sure way of finding out which of your acquaintances have the right values and which are more concerned with appearances than true friendship.

I have always believed that happiness is more important than money, but redundancy, unemployment and low pensions may cut a woman off from the very activities that would give her confidence, causing an even deeper sense of reserve in someone who was already inclined to be shy. I know several women who cannot afford the fees for evening classes and conferences, several who don't invite friends to meals because the cost of food has risen so steeply, others who can no longer run a car and can't go out to meet their friends in the evening because there is no bus service. Shortage of money can lead to loneliness as well as lack of confidence.

However, I firmly believe that ways can usually be found to improve a situation, given a positive approach, perseverance and a little imagination. I have never forgotten a saying of my father's that has proved itself true for me on countless occasions: 'When a door closes, a window opens'. Poverty can lead to new friend-ships, to the opportunity to help others in difficult situations and to the realization that money, important though it undoubtedly is, can't buy happiness; some of the richest people on earth are among the most miserable. If your poverty – or comparative poverty – is lowering your self-esteem, remember that the people who really matter in this life are the ones who love us for ourselves, regardless of our bank balance.

The following suggestions may be useful if you are short of

funds: make more use of your public library and listen to a wider range of radio programmes to discover new interests; write regular letters to give pleasure to some of the friends you normally contact only at Christmas; keep a diary, noting all the things that delight you and none that don't; sort out your photographs and add captions and dates for the benefit of young relatives; start an ambitious embroidery, knitting or patchwork project; learn a language; go to church; take up some long-forgotten activity such as water-colour painting, writing poetry, collecting stamps, making a herb garden or copying out favourite quotations. If none of these appeals, perhaps they will spark off something else. 'An hour of concentrated work,' said Benjamin Franklin, 'does more to kindle joy, to overcome sadness and set your ship afloat again, than a month of gloomy brooding.'

Guilt

This is such an important cause of shyness that I have given it a chapter all to itself (see page 71).

There are, of course, many other reasons I have not covered. If you can identify your own, I feel sure it will help you; there's no doubt that understanding the causes of any problem goes a long way to solving it.

5

Overcoming Self-consciousness

I'd like to share with you an important truth that I've discovered in more than half a century of striving to overcome my own self-consciousness: *the answer is within ourselves*. You may be very much aware of this already and those of you who are believers will know and love the message from the Bible: 'The Kingdom of Heaven is within you'. This belief is echoed in other great philosophies. No matter what caused your shyness in the first place, it's perfectly possible to put it all behind you, where it belongs. If you are prepared to face up to the challenge, you can look forward to a much more carefree life, to finding a fuller potential and being grateful for the blessings you have. We must all accept our limitations, but we cannot be sure what they are until every effort has been made.

Can shyness be overcome?

Yes, it can – at least, to a very large extent. I've proved it myself and dozens of my friends and students have won through to confidence and fulfilment after years of miserable self-consciousness. If your shyness is a very serious problem, keeping you indoors and virtually friendless, then you may need professional treatment. But when all is said and done, there is no-one who can help you better than yourself and you will have to discover by trial and error the methods that suit you best. Your progress towards self-confidence may be a gradual one (and I think we must all accept occasional attacks of shyness along with the other discomforts of life), but in a few weeks from now you could be a very much more relaxed and independent person.

The first thing is to tell yourself that you can and will succeed, venturing every day into some activity, however small, which has seemed to be a problem. A friend of mine called Josie always used to sit in the back row if she went to a lecture. (Sitting at the back is normal for shy people, as you probably know, although at school it can reveal a propensity for passing notes and eating sweets!) I advised Josie to sit further forward next time she went to a lecture, then further still until one day she would go bravely to the front. It worked, and once she had achieved this small triumph, she felt a new confidence in other fields as well. For instance, she now looks people in the eye when she talks to them and this, of course, is essential for a good rapport.

There are many ways in which you can train yourself to 'sit at the front' instead of hiding in the back row and, if you practise this approach, you will gradually feel more comfortable in your new role. We all want to 'be our own person', unhampered by needless apprehensions, and in most cases it is a prize we can win by our own determined efforts.

Everyone is shy

Everyone – but *everyone* – is shy to a certain extent. We wouldn't be human if we didn't have our 'tender spots', areas of sensitivity that can be hurt by a thoughtless remark or by any number of unforeseen circumstances. People who suffer from shyness sometimes fail to realize that those who seem self-confident are often trembling inside. Of course, there are many degrees of shyness and some lucky folk are indeed relatively free from it. But never totally. Many of us (and I am one of the confident-looking ones) have learnt to conceal our inner turmoils, to act as if we were self-assured when we are nothing of the kind. However, 'acting as if' can have remarkable results. No doubt you have felt depressed or under the weather before some important event when other people were relying on you to present a cheerful face. In order not to let them down, you have said nothing about your indisposition and acted as if you were feeling fine. After a while you probably *did* feel better; in fact, you may have forgotten all about it and thoroughly enjoyed yourself. 'Acting as if' is a splendid therapy. It is especially helpful if you are feeling self-conscious, and with perseverence it could eventually be replaced by *behaving* as if!

My creative writing students are mostly beginners and I help them to develop their talent by asking them to read out their work for constructive criticism. The atmosphere is friendly and informal but it can be very daunting for a shy person to come out in front of a class of fifteen strangers and read an exercise. Of course I never press them to do so if they are worried about it but it's remarkable how, after several evenings of seeing the more self-assured ones learning by it and even *enjoying* it, they volunteer to do likewise.

Ruth, a successful business woman, is beautiful, elegant and witty, and to see her at a party you'd think she had never known the meaning of shyness. And yet she confessed to me that she used to hate her appearance and never accepted party invitations. 'My shoulders are too broad and my hands are too big,' she complained. 'And my teeth are horribly uneven – surely you've noticed?' I hadn't. Her teeth might not be even but they give her a beguiling individuality because her smile is so warm. 'For heaven's sake, Ruth,' I said, 'we've all got bits of us that aren't perfect. It's the variations from the norm that make us unique.' She wasn't convinced, but later she got engaged and her fiancé obviously liked her as she was, so she began to accept herself. Sometimes we only need the approval of someone we respect to put things into perspective. It's sad that an unkind remark can damage a sensitive person's self-esteem more easily than a word of praise can build it up. We must try to accept the kindly comments we receive and disregard the critical ones unless they are friendly and constructive.

Concern for other people

It's odd that someone with Ruth's advantages should have felt unsure of herself because I know many women with serious disabilities who have a real excuse for lack of confidence, yet seem to be at home in the world. Self-confidence has a lot to do with self-esteem, of liking one's inner self, in a way that has nothing to do with physical attributes. People who care about others and don't pay too much attention to what people are

thinking about them can usually overcome their self-consciousness more easily than those who are inclined to be self-absorbed.
It's true to say, I think, that shyness is sometimes connected with
vanity! I know I've been guilty of this myself, especially in my
youth. Now I have learned from experience that a real concern
for other people can make one's inhibitions vanish like magic.
Can you imagine, for instance, being shy if someone fainted and
needed assistance? Yet those around us are constantly needing
our help in less dramatic ways; they need reassurance, comfort,
and a sympathetic listening ear.

Each day you can venture a little further into the world of self-
assurance: talking to your neighbour in the shopping queue (you
never know how lonely she may be), phoning an acquaintance
and inviting her for coffee or a drink, volunteering for hospital
visiting, or any of a dozen friendly overtures you have always
been too shy to initiate. Somewhere a start must be made and
you'll be amazed how much easier you feel about your personal
relationships once you have made the effort.

Don't belittle yourself

Another positive approach is to avoid self-deprecation. People
are inclined to become what they imagine themselves to be, and
every time we belittle ourselves we add to our sense of inferiority
and hamper our progress towards self-confidence. Sometimes, of
course, it's just a cry for reassurance; we want to be told that we
aren't as bad as we say we are! 'I'm hopeless at figures' is one of
my own perpetual cries and I really must put a stop to it. I *am*
hopeless at figures but most people are hopeless at something.
I'm no good at needlework either. I can hardly sew on a button
without stitching it to something it isn't meant to be stitched to!
Still, I'm a good cook and good at English, so let's concentrate on
our assets and not be afraid to congratulate ourselves occasionally. If you're inclined to underrate yourself it's a great help to
make a list of all your good points. Why not do it now? Write
down every positive attribute you can think of. (Do it alpha-
betically if you don't know where to start!) No-one need see it, so

you don't have to be modest and I'm sure you'll feel a great deal more confident when you read it over.

Self-deprecation can become a habit, so watch out for any downbeat remarks you make about yourself and put a stop to them. Nobody wants to hear me saying I'm hopeless at figures and needlework; it's boring. ('So what?' said an honest friend, and I think that was fair comment!)

Tender spots

Shyness, as we know, is mainly fear, and our tender spots can make us afraid of being hurt. I have a friend called Mrs Jarvis, a pleasant, middle-aged woman who is fond of gardening and passionately devoted to her three grandchildren. You'd never dream that she was shy. However, she told me that she dreads meeting strangers in case they mention Paris. Her husband was killed in a car crash there and she is afraid of betraying her distress.

I think we must try to accept these occasional hazards, knowing they are unavoidable if we are to live a normal life. Acceptance is the key word, as with all the problems of this world, when change is impossible. I have a favourite book called *The Wisdom of Insecurity* by Alan W. Watts. It seems a paradox but if we recognize the fact that insecurity is bound to be a part of the human state, then we see that it is wiser to accept it than to fight it.

I have a very tender spot myself. In 1983 our son died at the age of thirty-four. I have gradually come to terms with the loss but, as anyone bereaved knows only too well, there will always be reminders. At first I was very much afraid of these in case I suddenly burst into tears for no apparent reason, but now I have learnt to accept them as an inescapable part of my life. We all have to cope with painful reminders of some kind or other and we must deal with them as wisely and cheerfully as we can. It's far from easy but there is always something to be grateful for and, provided we can avoid self-pity, life has all manner of joy and fulfilment to offer.

One of our greatest enemies – an enemy that can hamper our progress in every direction – is lethargy. We must combat this tendency if we are to live the happy and rewarding life we all long for.

Fighting lethargy

Shyness can lead us into lethargy unless we guard against it. That hopeless feeling of isolation, of being unable to enjoy parties and discussions, make new friends and engage wholeheartedly in the activities we secretly long for, can cause a sense of futility, and a desire to opt out. In overcoming lethargy we can take a big step on the way to conquering our shyness. Lethargy is a destructive state of mind and, because of its negative nature, it gets in the way of its own cure. It loves to see us sink even lower into that time-wasting, debilitating pit. How, then, are we to cast it off and set ourselves free to spend those precious hours on some rewarding activity? In almost every case, it *can* be overcome and there are many ways of doing it.

My method is self-interest. I have, like most of us, a very strong desire for happiness and peace of mind; I know that if I slump in a chair, achieving nothing, helping nobody, I shall grow more and more disgusted with myself and end up thoroughly miserable. And so, nine times out of ten (we'll talk about the tenth in a minute), I manage to make the effort to 'get up and get on'. And we all know the importance of that first move. If you've got a door to paint you have only to take the lid off the paint-can and you're away. But that initial effort can be extremely difficult. Sometimes it helps if we picture the goal we wish to accomplish: the door, gleaming with fresh paint; a cake golden-brown from the oven; a newly-weeded border; the pleasure of a friend when he or she receives a letter from us. For me, the goal is usually a pile of typescript, finally corrected and ready for the publisher. Whatever the task that faces you, imagine the satisfaction of knowing it is done and tell yourself that you will make a start on it *right now*.

But what about that tenth time, when no amount of good

intentions can get you out of your chair – or out of bed? Lethargy seems to be a combination of fatigue and depression: part physical, part mental. Sometimes you're feeling low because you've been overworking or battered by some personal problem. In this case, a short holiday or a programme of deep relaxation can work wonders. Fresh air and a healthy diet are important, too. If your inertia is so persistent that you can do nothing to overcome it, you should perhaps consult your doctor and make sure there is no physical cause that needs attention. But most of the time, we simply need a different attitude of mind – a positive attitude that knows where it wants to go and is determined to get there.

Fear of failure can be a problem. If you can face up to this, recalling your past successes and resolving to persevere against all odds, the blockage may soon be removed. Anxiety, as most of us know to our cost, can drain us of energy. If we are burdened with some other problem apart from shyness, it's quite common to find ourselves a prey to lethargy. Sometimes only time can provide the solution, but let's make sure we aren't delaying our recovery by a kind of reluctance to return to normality. Perhaps –quite naturally – we are craving for sympathy? Maybe, if someone is around, we are hoping to be offered cups of tea, a shoulder to cry on, a patient listening ear? Caring friends can help a great deal, unless they coddle us too much, but to earn the respect of those we love – and perhaps what is more important, our self-respect – we must make the effort ourselves. 'It's up to me!' is a favourite maxim of mine, and if I say the words aloud it often does the trick.

When you feel so lacking in drive that you can't drag yourself out of your chair, take a deep breath, count three and force yourself to stand up. Then make the first move to start the job in hand. It may be lighting the oven to do some cooking, putting on your gardening shoes, getting out the writing pad or the needlework box. Whatever it is, if you can make that one big effort to start, you will probably find that in half an hour you'll be so deeply involved that you won't want to stop.

It doesn't matter how trivial the task; once the action has

begun, even in a very small way, our inertia is conquered and we are heading for freedom. Do something to cheer yourself up. Or, better still, something to cheer up someone else. Phoning a friend who might be lonely has often changed my mood from self-pitying stupor to lively engagement; a caring little chat can work miracles. But however you solve the problem, you will find that success breeds success, as in every endeavour. When you manage to make the effort, the next time will be easier. And so it goes on. Gradually you will form the habit of satisfying work, and those dreary, unproductive days will be a thing of the past. This will help to build up your self-esteem; a poor self-image, as we have seen, is one of the main reasons for timidity.

You will, of course, have your own personal solution to the problem of lethargy but for me the reading of some well-loved book can be a source of strength and inspiration. It may be a religious work, a book of poems, a novel or a textbook on a favourite subject. Contact with an author of our choice can often revive the flagging spirit and set us on our way with renewed enthusiasm. Likewise, listening to music. I wouldn't advise watching television; unless the programme is of very special interest you can sink into even deeper lethargy. But you don't need me to tell you that!

Another tip is to set a deadline for the completion of a project and tell someone you respect that nothing will keep you from fulfilling it. In this way you can shame yourself into action. The approval of those we care for can be a marvellous incentive.

Unless you are a heavy morning sleeper, an early start can help. Some people groan aloud at the mere idea and, if you are one of them, you can probably function late at night. It's all a question of how we are made. After splashing my face with cold water and enjoying a cup of tea I'm more ready for work at 6 a.m. than I would have been at eight; no-one will ring the doorbell, no-one will phone. Those early hours, when the mind is clear and unfatigued, can be a godsend.

Exercise is a wonderful remedy. A brisk walk in the open air – or a work-out indoors on a wet day – can release the natural anti-depressants in the body and make us feel much better. For me, there is also something curative in the very sights and sounds of nature.

In a later chapter I shall talk about relaxation and how we can use the subconscious mind to free us from all kinds of fears and anxieties. Shyness and relaxation don't mix. If we can learn to let go of our tensions we are well on the way to serenity and self-reliance.

6

Women have Special Problems

When I was invited to write this book I said, 'Why a *woman's* guide? Men are shy as well!' And, of course, they are. This book, however, is designed as one of a series on women's problems and there's no getting away from the fact that we do have special difficulties. I love being a woman but I often feel incensed by the chauvinistic attitude of some of the men I know; I can see how their behaviour undermines the confidence of the women in their lives.

Second-class citizens

We all know that women have traditionally been treated as second-class citizens. ('The male is by nature superior and the female inferior; the one rules and the other is ruled,' said Aristotle, who should have known better!) No matter how enlightened our families may have been in giving us the respect and freedom we need, we shall always come across the occasional domineering man who will take pleasure in putting us down merely because we are female. Sadly, there are many women who are unwilling or unable to stand up for their rights, whether in the home or in society at large. If we study the problems and relate them to our own situation, we are in a stronger position to resist injustice. Many wives seem to accept the role of the Uncomplaining Little Woman and invite victimization. There lies the path to lack of self-esteem and its inevitable bedfellow, shyness.

Right from the start, girls are on a sticky wicket. 'It's a boy!' is the usual ecstatic cry from everyone around (except perhaps the mother) at the birth of a son. In other words, 'Hurray, it isn't a girl!' No wonder we are conditioned from the word Go to consider ourselves inferior. (Some Asian women seek an abortion if a daughter is forecast but this is probably the

42

husband's decision anyway!) We must continually remind our-selves that we have no real reason to feel inferior; we only *think* we have.

Many parents, of course, are equally delighted by the arrival of a son or a daughter – all they want is a healthy baby of either sex – but I can remember my mother saying wistfully to me when I was quite small: 'I really wanted a boy – we were going to call you John.' I was christened Joan but I never liked the name, perhaps for that reason. At the age of seventeen I chose the name Dianne for myself and have used it ever since. That's a secret cat out of the bag because I've told hardly anyone up till now. Writing this book is obviously going to get rid of some of my own inhibitions as well as yours!

However pleased our parents might be to have us, brothers and boys at school show sexual discrimination at a very early age. 'Go away – we don't want *girls* playing with us!' '*You* can't do it – you're a *girl*!' 'Girls can't play cricket – they can't *throw*.' And in many cases that's true. The inferior physical strength of the average girl compared with her male counterpart can hamper her achievement and result in lack of confidence, but it has nothing whatever to do with her innate quality as a person.

Many women have very soft voices and this can lead to shyness. I knew a very reserved woman in a writers' group who wrote beautifully but always wanted someone else to read out her stories because she couldn't produce sufficient volume to be heard by everybody in the room. Then she went to an elocution class and improved so much that eventually she was able to read her own work and felt much more self-assured.

Girls are often treated by their parents with less respect than their brothers. They may not be expected to demand higher education ('She'll get married anyway!'). Sometimes they are not allowed to pursue the career that attracts them. A friend of mine passionately wanted to go to drama school when she was young but her parents wouldn't hear of it; they didn't think the stage was a suitable vocation for their daughter.

Lack of achievement is a factor that creates a great deal of reticence. Conversely, it often happens that even a small success can dispel those niggling doubts about oneself. I felt a great deal more confident when my first novel was published and I have a friend who seemed to lose her shyness overnight when she won the first prize in a big photographic competition. Economic dependence is another factor; how can a woman feel secure and self-possessed if she has to ask her husband for the money to buy him a birthday present?

If you feel rather lacking in achievement, why not make a serious attempt to branch out into something new?

Discovering hidden talents

Everyone has a talent of some kind, if only he or she can discover it. Some find out in later life that they possess surprising gifts. Whatever your age and background, if you are not aware of your own special ability, why not seek it out and develop it? It could do a great deal for your self-confidence.

If you feel you have no talent for anything, please think again. You may need to make a sustained effort before you discover the delight of an unexpected interest and you don't have to become an expert to derive great pleasure from it.

Shyness is often the reason why the years pass by and skills remain undiscovered. If, in the past, someone has made you feel unsure of yourself, try to put it out of your mind and make an independent assessment, free from any previous sense of inferiority. To succeed in anything, we need a measure of confidence and, once we have it, even to a small degree, the wheels begin to turn and anything can happen. 'A man who is self-reliant, positive, optimistic and undertakes his work with the assurance of success, magnetises his condition. He draws to himself the creative powers of the universe.' (*The Power of Positive Thinking* by Norman Vincent Peale.)

— Don't be afraid of failure. People who never make mistakes, never make anything! Above my writing desk is a card that says 'TRIAL AND ERROR ARE PART OF THE TASK'. This is to remind me that there is nothing to worry about when my waste-paper basket overflows with screwed-up pages of unsatisfactory writing. One often has to write a chapter half-a-dozen times to get it right. Trial and error are part of every worthwhile skill – cooking, sewing, playing a musical instrument, learning to drive a car. . . .

The subjects you enjoyed at school are naturally a useful guide, but if you ask yourself what you were doing with your spare time as a child under ten, before the examination system got you into its clutches, you might find an even clearer directive. I myself was writing poems and stories. A friend who is now a dressmaker was already cutting up remnants of material and tacking bits together when she was seven. Musicians can usually trace their gifts back to childhood. Organizers start organizing in the playground. So try to remember what you most enjoyed. Were you drawing, inventing things, writing, working out figures, crazy about some sport or hobby, devoted to animals, comforting people. . . ? Were you a loner or a mixer? A dreamer or a doer? If you're very shy you were probably a loner and a dreamer. Now is the time to make your dreams reality. Your talents may not bring you fame or fortune but they could bring you enormous satisfaction. And never let us underrate the basic talents of homemaking: cooking, gardening, sewing, interior decoration or the flair for helping children (one's own or other people's) to be happy and fulfilled.

The need to earn a living drives many people to pursue the kind of work they would not otherwise choose, leading to frustration and stress. It may not be possible to change but we can usually arrange to spend a little time on something closer to our hearts; the effort will be rewarded in terms of pleasure and sometimes in profit as well. A friend of mine works in a bank because her father pushed her into it many years ago. She hates every minute but now, with so much unemployment, she dare not risk a change. However, her true bent is creative writing and she gets up every morning at six o'clock to work on a novel. One day she might get it published but, even if she doesn't, the work has given her a great deal of satisfaction.

The following exercise has proved useful to many who lacked

the motivation to learn a new skill. First of all, write down an impossible dream – something you long to achieve but know you never will; for example, to play on the Centre Court at Wimbledon, to win the Nobel Prize for Literature or to speak French like a native. Secondly, write down a possible goal related to your dream. And thirdly, a step towards that goal which you could take *tomorrow*.

Let's say you long to speak French like a native. A possible aim would be to speak it well enough to make yourself understood. Tomorrow you could find out about French classes in your area, buy or borrow books and tapes and make a start.

Here are some further headings. Prepare a list of your own to suit whatever impossible dream you have in mind (which is, of course, a valuable clue to your particular bent), and you may well be on the way to discovering a hidden talent.

1. To win the Nobel Prize for Literature.
2. To have an article or short story accepted for publication.
3. Join a Writers' Circle or class, get some books on the subject and start writing seriously. My own paperback textbooks *Teach Yourself Creative Writing* and *The Craft of Novel-Writing* might be helpful to would-be writers.

1. To be a TV cook.
2. To pass a Cordon Bleu Course.
3. Study your cookery books, practise new recipes and find out about local classes.

1. To play the organ at Westminster Abbey.
2. To play in your local church.
3. Arrange for music lessons.

Since giving talks along these lines, I have heard from several students who found creative outlets as a result of the 'list of three'. One has joined a dancing class (Famous Ballerina), one is learning First Aid (Top Surgeon), and another is working at a crèche (Child Psychologist). Aim high and you will clear the rooftops even if you never reach the moon. Incidentally, a would-be actress who joined a dramatic society and volunteered for scene-painting, discovered an artistic talent she knew nothing about and now shows her pictures at local art exhibitions. So it isn't always our childhood interests that follow through to later life; one thing can lead to another, and all manner of pleasant surprises lie in wait for us if we will only make the effort to invite them.

If, after all, no special aptitude presents itself, you could find great satisfaction in working for a cause you care about – perhaps through voluntary service – or by helping someone not to be lonely. This kind of activity may, in its turn, lead you to discover in yourself a gift, hitherto unrecognized, of listening patiently to unhappy people and giving them hope and encouragement. And that is surely one of the greatest talents of all.

Biological problems

Menstruation tops the bill, I suppose. Not only the pains and inconvenience, not only the misery of pre-menstrual tension (and later the menopause) but the sheer *indignity* of it all. When I was first going out with my husband-to-be, my period arrived unexpectedly, staining the back of my tropical khaki skirt (we were both in the RAF in Cairo). He was the one who had to tell me about it and, although he was very sweet and understanding, I couldn't help but be embarrassed and – quite illogically – ashamed. Yes, women do indeed have special problems!

Our submissive role in the sexual act is inescapable. We can be made pregnant against our will. We can be raped. We can also suffer miscarriages, Caesarean births, abortions, hysterectomies, mastectomies and many other exclusively female traumas. All this, you may quite rightly be thinking, is because we have the amazing, glorious and miraculous power of *giving birth*. Nevertheless, that marvellous gift can have its negative side, making a woman feel as if the whole world is against her simply because she was designed for reproducing the species.

If we feed our babies ourselves, as we know is best for them, we are in regular demand, day in, day out, for months on end. Even though we may love it and wouldn't have things any

WOMEN HAVE SPECIAL PROBLEMS

different, motherhood often means relinquishing a satisfying career.

Career versus marriage

For a man there is seldom a clash, but for a woman it may necessitate doing two full-time jobs: coping with the home in addition to her career. If her partner is willing and able to help with the shopping, cooking and cleaning, the burden is eased, but this is the exception rather than the rule and the woman may become overtired and discontented. Hardly a recipe for self-confidence.

I've had this problem for most of my married life: full-time writing in addition to the tasks of a housewife. When I'm scraping the carrots I'm planning the next chapter. When I'm revising a difficult paragraph I'm half aware that I ought to be going to the shops or starting the lunch. Or it *used* to be like that. I've now discovered that when my two lives are in conflict I can function better if I concentrate on one thing at a time. Frustration and resentment were undermining my happiness. Now I try, when I'm doing the chores, not to fret about the writing I could be doing. And when I'm working I steer my mind away from the cooking and cleaning. 'Dividing the day into manageable portions,' said Robert Louis Stevenson, 'brings peace of mind and healthful activity to the body.' Absolutely right – but he was a man, of course!

In spite of being fairly 'liberated' I can't quite get it out of my head that I ought to be a housewife first and a writer second. My head says 'No!' but my heart says 'Yes' – though in an undertone! If I go on typing so long that there isn't time to make a casserole for dinner, I feel *guilty*. It isn't my husband's fault – he couldn't be more sympathetic – it's the old-age conditioning that 'a woman's place is in the home', and it needs an awful lot of re-conditioning to get rid of it. If there are children, of course, they must come first and a career might have to wait until they reach school age, but at least we can utilize those years in preparation for the work we have in mind. When my son was small I used to get up at 4.30 a.m. to write (I was struggling to get into print in those days) because that was the only time I was free; I was too tired by the evening. But I did manage to serve my apprenticeship during those early hours and if I hadn't done *something*, I know I'd have lost confidence in myself. It may not be easy but if we are going to establish (or preserve) a good self-image after marriage, we must find the courage to pursue the career of our choice, in spite of the difficulties.

It may be that a married woman has no wish for a career outside the home. In this case it saddens me when I hear her say, 'Oh, I'm only a housewife' if someone asks her what she does. Being a housewife is a wonderfully creative and worthwhile job and needs no apologies. The only danger is becoming so deeply involved in domesticity that she ceases to be a stimulating companion to her husband and friends. When a woman has small children to look after and can't go out in the evenings unless a baby-sitter can be arranged, she may lose confidence, especially if her husband doesn't properly understand her frustration. She should try to make friends with other young mothers so that they can share the baby-sitting and help one another to achieve a certain amount of freedom.

Loneliness

Widows and divorcees often complain that they seldom get invited to parties, whereas a man on his own is in great demand. I was touched by Karen Blixen's remark in the film *Out of Africa*: 'Men go off to be tested for courage and, if we're tested at all, it's for patience, for doing without, for how long we can endure loneliness.'

One solution is to invite an acquaintance for a meal. A simple buffet supper is all you need, and you'll give pleasure and deepen a friendship as a result. I suggested this to a lonely widow and she said that no-one would want to come and see her because she wasn't interesting enough. I was amazed! She has travelled widely, has plenty to say (but is not boring) and is an excellent cook. Added to which, she never moans and has a good sense of humour. This kind of self-denigration is at the root of many women's shyness, and they miss out on giving pleasure as well as receiving it because of a mistaken idea of their own short-comings.

Many women feel uneasy about going into a restaurant or bar by themselves, although the situation today has greatly improved and one often sees women on their own. I don't mind going for a lone drink or a meal – so long as I have the rewarding company of a book to read or a notebook to write in.

Last year I spent a glorious week in Venice by myself. I'm lucky to have a husband who doesn't make me feel guilty if I leave him on his own occasionally but if you aren't so lucky, I still recommend you to break loose from time to time if you possibly can. I made some good friends in the hotel but most of the time I was alone, reading and writing and sight-seeing and taking photographs. Some people are by nature more self-contained and independent than others but shy women need company and reassurance. They really should go out and about on their own and make new friends. Some time ago I managed to persuade a divorced woman to book a package holiday to Crete. She had a marvellous time and is saving up for another lone trip next year.

I'll tell you a little anecdote about loneliness. Many years ago, in my shy days, I felt very miserable at a cocktail party standing alone with my drink while a throng of people laughed and chattered around me. I felt as if everyone must be scorning me for having no companion. Then later I went to a similar party with a man friend and stood alone while he went off for a few minutes to make a phone call. From everyone else's point of view my situation was exactly the same, but I wasn't in the least bit uneasy. Isn't it a question of how we feel within ourselves, quite regardless of what others might be thinking of us? It would be just the same if a boyfriend failed to turn up and left you standing outside a cinema or a disco. If he really had stood you up you'd feel as if everyone knew, whereas if he had just gone off to buy you a box of chocolates you'd feel great. The truth of the matter, of course, is that people are usually far too much involved with their own lives to wonder why we are on our own. We feel less self-conscious when we stop imagining that everyone is looking at us; unless we're famous or fabulously beautiful or dressed outrageously, they aren't!

— You can usually solve the problem of loneliness at a party by looking out for someone else who is alone and making the effort to talk to them. Men are often shy as well and would welcome a friendly overture. You might also go round with a plate of goodies or ask your hostess if there's anything else you can do to help.

All these examples will have shown you (as if you didn't know already!) that we have plenty of reasons for an inferiority complex on account of our gender alone and, if we are to counteract the damage, we must dig our heels in very firmly. We need to assess the problems before we can solve them, and the fact that you are taking the trouble to read this book is a big step in the right direction.

7

Shyness with Men

This is perhaps the most distressing aspect of shyness a woman has to face. Most of us want to make a good impression on the opposite sex; it starts in the nursery and can last till our dying day. It's right and natural and necessary. Men feel the same about women; members of the opposite sex play a vital part in most of our lives. How else would the race continue?

And so it is very important for women to overcome their shyness and establish good and easy relationships with the men they meet. One day – almost inevitably – they will fall in love and too much shyness can delay, or even destroy, the happiness they dream of. A certain degree of reticence may be quite in order but shyness is infectious and, if the man is unsure of himself as well, the relationship might never develop as both parties would like.

When we are adolescents it is natural, because of the mystique and excitement of sex, to blush when we think a boy is looking at us, to be tongue-tied when he talks to us – or to answer brusquely when that is the last thing we really want to do. As adults, too, many women feel a certain apprehension until they have found the right partner. Every eligible bachelor is a possible candidate but I think it is wise to put this out of our minds as far as possible and try to achieve friendship before expecting romance. The sexual scene is charged with drama and danger, as well as latent passion and glorious expectations, so it isn't easy to feel calm and confident. Some women are very shy indeed; some go to the other extreme and hurl themselves at every man they meet. Obviously we must try to find the right balance.

In this chapter I am really addressing myself to women whose shyness gets in the way of rewarding friendships. Why do we sometimes frighten away the very man we most wish to attract, making him think we are unimpressed or even antagonistic?

A domineering father can make a girl distrust all men. A brother who taunted and teased us to excess, a boyfriend who humiliated us or left us for another girl, a bad marriage or an unhappy love affair of any kind – all these things can instil a fear of being hurt again and damage our relationships unless we resolve to welcome each new man into our lives entirely on his own merit.

The way we look

Perhaps the most common reason for shyness is uncertainty of our power to win a man's attentions. We think we are not pretty enough, too fat, too thin, too tall, too short, too ignorant, too dull. . . . A good self-image is essential if we are to overcome our shyness with men, or with anyone else. Think of the women you know who have happy marriages; are they all brilliant and beautiful, with perfect figures and exquisite grooming? Not on your life! Conventional beauty may attract a man in the first place – and of course good looks are an advantage – but if a pretty girl turns out to be selfish, mean and arrogant, her physical charms won't keep him happy for long. A strikingly beautiful woman may have a shyness problem just *because* she looks so stunning. She may be anxious lest she is receiving attention on account of her looks rather than her personality.

I recently read a survey in a women's magazine in which a dozen famous and charming men were invited to list the qualities they found most attractive in women. Top three on the list were kindness, a sense of humour and *self-confidence*. None of these has any connection with outward appearances, except that kindliness and humour lend a warm light to a woman's eyes.

I think the advertisements for clothes and make-up conspire to foster a feeling of inadequacy in many women who know they don't measure up to the glamorous models who wear the goods on offer. Isn't it better to forget the ads and give your attention to those aspects of your personality that *really* matter? Of course we should try to look our best because it gives us confidence – and out of respect for our companions – but if we set our standards too high, most of us are bound to be disappointed. Go back to that list of your positive attributes you made in Chapter 5 (if you didn't make one, why not do it now?). If we don't have a reasonably good opinion of ourselves we shall always have difficulty in relating to other people; most men, although they warm to modest and unofficious women, find shyness very hard to cope with.

Sex

The fear of sex is obviously another important reason for timidity. This may have been caused by an assault in childhood or adolescence, or by a previous experience with a man who was clumsy, selfish or violent in his love-making. Or it may arise from an upbringing which taught us that sexual satisfaction for women is unnecessary or even wrong. Religion is often the cause; we may feel that we don't deserve the happiness and fulfilment we long for. The warning we quite rightly received in childhood about the dangers of strange men must also be a factor.

Loving contact is important in all our relationships and some women find it difficult to touch another person *at all* – never mind a man! You may be inclined to shrink away when people show their affection in a physical way, and responsibility for this kind of reticence could lie with parents who never kissed or cuddled you as a child. If the prospect of sexual intercourse causes you concern, or even alarm, then of course you are shy with men, and the tragic spread of Aids is bound to increase your anxiety. Ignorance plays a large part in causing inhibitions but there are many excellent books on sale that cover all aspects of sex; if you are too shy to buy one in a shop your doctor will advise you on reliable literature by mail order.

We may know the reasons for our inhibitions but how on earth are we to be rid of them?

Men are not so different

A lot of our shyness is due to the fact that we think of men as totally different from ourselves, and we shall feel much easier in their company if we remember that they have the same needs as us for love and fulfilment, for self-confidence and peace of mind. Most men long for a permanent and loving relationship, just as we do, and continued philandering is often a search for the woman who can fulfil this longing. They want to be comforted when things go wrong; they need sympathy and understanding; they are, in most cases, no less sensitive and easily hurt than we are but because of their stiff-upper-lip conditioning they feel constrained to hide their emotions. If we bear in mind that women usually have a special built-in toughness (bestowed on us, no doubt, to enable us to withstand the strain of childbirth) and that men are, in many cases, weaker and more easily discouraged than we are, we are much less likely to be shy of them.

If we could read the thoughts of the average man we would probably find that they run along much the same lines as ours do (with a few obvious exceptions!). They have secret anxieties about their health, about money, children and household matters. And about the threat of nuclear war. To understand this, and to *show* that we understand it, is bound to reduce our shyness.

We mustn't forget that our sexual attractions, whether we are aware of them or not, may disturb the men we meet, making them uneasy; their embarrassment can make us feel we have done something wrong when all we have done is to be our normal, female selves. We can't overlook the fact that some men are 'only after one thing', but I believe that trust is an essential part of true friendship. Suspicion, though sometimes justified, is a negative and unattractive quality. And it certainly leads to a wary kind of shyness.

Single-sex schools can, of course, lead to shyness with boys unless a girl has brothers. Myra, a friend of mine educated at a girls' school, said that she hardly dared to speak to a boy when she left. She is now happily married and has some good advice to offer. She thinks it's important to persevere in situations you find intimidating. 'If you feel you *ought* to be able to cope,' she said, 'don't opt out! Make a real effort to overcome your inhibitions.

When I left school I had to force myself to talk to young men and it gradually became easier.'

Six helpful hints

1. Be sure to accept compliments gracefully

I overheard this exchange at a party.

HE: That's a lovely dress you're wearing.

SHE: Oh, this old thing – I've had it for ages and it needs cleaning anyway.

The poor man felt snubbed and lost interest, making the woman even less self-assured. The best response to a compliment is a happy smile and a 'Thank you'.

2. Beware of apologizing too much

If you're unavoidably late, say you're sorry, of course, but don't go on and on with boring explanations and excuses. Some women seem to apologize for being alive ('Pardon me for breathing!' as Basil Brush would say) and if you catch yourself saying 'Sorry' when there's really no need for it, this is an area to watch. I've heard women apologize for having doors slammed in their faces and their feet trodden on. It's a familiar psychological problem and it revolves round a woman's feeling that everything must be *her fault*. ('Did I keep you waiting?' when she wasn't even late; 'Are you *sure* you don't mind?' when she's asking for something perfectly reasonable.) It stems from a poor self-image and is very closely related to shyness. Most men find it irritating and their irritation confirms the woman's conviction that she isn't liked or likable.

3. Don't be over-considerate

I know several women who never do what *they* want to do but invariably insist on their companions taking whatever advantages are going. ('No, *you* sit by the window.' 'No, *you* have the one with the cherry.' 'No, *I'll* carry that.') It may be said that this attitude reflects a laudable desire to please, but taken to excess it is hardly endearing. It seems as if the woman in question is saying between the lines: 'Look how unselfish I am!' Women of this kind usually take unkindly to criticism and this is another well-known sign of a poor self-image. They set too high a standard for themselves, fail to reach it and don't want to be reminded of their imperfections.

4. *Make a real effort to communicate with the men you meet*

Ask for their opinions and offer your own. Don't be afraid of appearing stupid or ignorant; the men will love to put you right! Ask questions, listen attentively and resolve to extend your interests. I enjoy watching football but I never quite understood the offside rule until I came across a man who was only too pleased to explain. Keep off domesticity unless you are talking to a reverse-role husband or a man who cooks. (I once had a marvellous time at a party exchanging recipes with a bank manager!) There are endless subjects to discuss: gardening, cars, books, music, television and radio, the latest big news story. . . . The main thing is not to talk about yourself too much – at least not at first!

5. *Remember that you can't expect everyone to like you*

It's quite an honour to be disliked by certain people! The women who never make enemies at all are usually so eager to please that they are over-accommodating and lack the courage of their convictions. I think we earn more respect if we are prepared to stand up for the things we believe in, however unpopular it may make us in certain quarters. To do so is a valuable lesson in overcoming shyness.

6. *Make allowances*

We have seen that men have more in common with women than is generally believed, but we must accept that there are many fundamental differences in attitude and do our best to be tolerant of these differences. Almost all men hate shopping, unless it's for something of their own, and sometimes not even then. It's torture for them to stand about while we make up our minds what kind of tights to buy or if we should try yet another shop before we decide on that skirt. Women, on the other hand, usually like shopping and are quite patient even when a man spends ages choosing a hack-saw or a camera lens.

Some men, however, need to assert their masculinity to such an extent that they frighten us to death. Unless you enjoy this kind of thing (and of course some women do!), I'd say it was best to steer clear. Tolerance, in such a case, might be too much to expect.

To sum up, keep in mind that men feel unsure of themselves as well, although they might not show it. If you can build up their self-esteem (while avoiding flattery and insincerity), you will feel much more at ease in their company. Your shyness will diminish if you can put aside your general anxieties about the male sex, remember that a man is innocent until he is proved guilty, and revel in the intriguing exercise of getting to know how the other half lives!

8

From Schoolgirl to Senior Citizen

As we go through life we are constantly meeting situations which can make us shy unless we guard against them. As children we can hardly defend ourselves but as we grow older we can do a great deal to minimize the damage if we understand the causes. In the first section of this chapter I shall be speaking not only to those who are shy themselves, but also to those who have dealings with young people.

The formative years

Little children are often shy merely because they are so small. Who could wonder at it? They are surrounded by adults who tower above them, shout at them, slap them, tell them to be quiet, to keep still, to do this and stop that, eat this, put that down. . . . And this applies to children who are loved and cherished. Think of the ones who are neglected or abused.

Many children are shy. Babies haven't yet learnt to be, but self-consciousness soon sets in. If you smile at a little girl of three you might be lucky enough to receive a smile in return but, more often than not, the child will turn away, put a hand to her mouth or hide behind her mother. Adults who talk about children above their heads, saying 'She's shy, you know', tend to make them even more self-conscious. Also, children of school age can feel put down when their parents call the person who stays with them a 'baby-sitter'. I remember making this mistake with our own son when he was about seven. 'I'm not a *baby*!' he exclaimed indignantly. From then on we changed the word to 'sitter-in' and I do recommend it.

I expect you can remember your own schooldays very clearly, however far away from them you may be. This shows how deeply they affect our lives and how vigilant we must be to counteract and try to disperse the negative influences we may have received.

Fear and anxiety are at the root of childish reticence, and parents can do a great deal to help by building up self-confidence right from the start. I think it's very important for everyone who has contact with children to praise them and trust them whenever possible.

We should never imbue children with fear and anxiety unless it is essential for their own safety and protection. Make them feel good. Make them feel clever and lovable. Make complimentary remarks about their appearance to give them a pride in the way they look. The seeds of shyness may have been sown by others but at least we can do everything in our power to make sure that those seeds receive no nourishment and are given no room to grow. This doesn't mean, of course, that we shan't be driven to blow our tops from time to time, but we must surely strive to make sure that nothing we say or do will add to the basic insecurity people feel simply because they are children. The danger lies in how we may behave when we are tired or unwell or under stress. It is dreadfully easy to seem angry or impatient with a child (or a partner, for that matter!) when, in reality, we are angry with ourselves. Partners can usually survive, but a child may become nervous or withdrawn if bombarded with too much criticism. A parent's voice, raised in anger, can cause psycho-logical damage to a small child who does not understand what she has done wrong. A guilt complex can begin at a very early age and, as the child grows older, any kind of criticism may seem to signify a lack of love and be taken too seriously.

There is also the problem of academic failures. A girl who does not shine at certain subjects may feel extremely shy in the classroom, constantly dreading the lessons she cannot properly understand. She will feel inadequate compared with brainy children and, unless she receives extra support and encourage-ment, this sense of inferiority can lead to a lack of self-esteem.

Bullying by other children can cause immense problems for those of a nervous disposition, and we all know that it isn't only boys who can be bullies! It's very important for children to feel that they have someone to turn to when they are subjected to any kind of intimidation – someone who will listen patiently and uncritically and offer practical assistance when it is needed. If you know a child who may be in need of a sympathetic ear, why not offer it without delay? You never know how vital this gesture may be.

Communication with a caring friend is essential at every age and in every difficult situation, but surely never more important than in childhood, when adults are often too busy to attend sufficiently to the pleas of a very small person.

There is probably no time of life so fraught with insecurity and shyness as the years between eleven and sixteen, when one is neither a child nor an adult. The onset of menstruation, often without previous knowledge (my mother never told me a thing and I thought I was *dying*!), can cause a deep sense of anxiety, quite apart from the physical aches and pains. Practical information, calmly and sympathetically offered with no tendency to cause alarm, can make all the difference. These days, thank goodness, we are much less secretive about our natural functions but many girls still start to menstruate without being properly informed beforehand. And, in any case, as we all know, it doesn't exactly boost our morale.

Puppy fat or excessive skinniness are important causes of shyness. So is acne. So is the development of our breasts and a fear that they might turn out to be too big or too small. Many of the pains of adolescence revolve around love and, as we all remember, our passions at that age, however short-lived, are no less deeply felt than those of an adult, whether they be directed towards a boy of our own age, a master at school, a pop star or the head girl!

I have a special interest in adolescents and I wrote seven novels for teenage girls in the 1970s. The dozens of friendly letters I received from my readers showed me how much girls in that age-group need and appreciate the sympathy and understanding of adults. Time after time I read the same messages from girls in Britain and the United States: 'Thank goodness *somebody* understands!' and 'Thank heaven I'm not the only one!' The themes of my novels related mainly to problems with boyfriends and parents. Parents, as I have already discussed, can undermine our self-confidence if they upbraid us too much, frustrate our ambitions or keep us from the friends we care for. And however sympathetic a girl's parents may be, they can cause her great anxiety if they are constantly quarrelling. Children with an unstable background can easily become either withdrawn or unruly unless they have the benefit of a caring adult to confide in.

Teenagers, especially if they are of a quiet disposition, dread going home to a disruptive atmosphere and, if they are driven away, they might become involved with other youngsters who have a dangerous influence. A girl of seventeen called Kathryn became so deeply upset by the growing friction between her domineering father and gentle mother that she left home and went to live with her boyfriend in an inner-city slum. In many ways she was happier than she had been in her comfortable suburban home, but she was tormented by other anxieties: fear of pregnancy, guilt over rejecting her parents, and the gradual realization that she didn't love her boyfriend enough to stay with him permanently. Now she is back at home. Her father has left for good to live with another woman, and the responsibility of comforting her mother and settling into a new job is helping Kathryn to achieve a new maturity. Added to this, she is now going out with a new man who is loving and supportive.

We all know the hazards of drugs, smoking and alcohol, not to mention the fear of Aids. Another problem is that many girls today are afraid that if they refuse to sleep with a boy they may lose him. They need the assurance that any boy who would reject a girl on that account is unlikely to be a very rewarding partner. Fear of unemployment may also threaten her peace of mind and can lead to the kind of wariness and reserve that we call shyness. If you are dealing with youngsters you will understand how vital it is to encourage them to discuss their problems and help them towards the confidence and security they need.

Perhaps you are under twenty yourself, undergoing a stressful time? If so, do make a real effort to talk out your troubles with a sympathetic relative, teacher or friend; it can make such a difference. If you find this impossible, there are addresses and telephone numbers at the end of this book to help you make contact with someone who will listen patiently to your side of the story. Remember that thousands of girls are going through similar experiences and if you have made a mistake, however serious, don't be afraid to admit it and ask for advice.

Things can change for the better quite unexpectedly, as they did for Kathryn; if you can weather the present storm you could be feeling a great deal happier very soon.

The prime of life

It's hardly surprising that many young women are anxious about the future. Shy or not, they have all kinds of problems to contend with: envy of prettier or more successful women, fears about health and housing, sexual problems, parents or grandparents, money. . . . A sense of insecurity or inadequacy can undermine their confidence just at the time when they feel they should have everything going for them. And so they should, in a saner and juster world. As things are, we can do no more than make the most of our opportunities, work towards a positive attitude, however daunting things might seem, and do what we can to ease the burdens of those with more serious problems than our own.

What practical advice, therefore, can I offer to those young women who are lacking in confidence and find a positive approach extremely difficult?

First of all, remind yourself that there are countless women who feel hopeless and frustrated, especially if they have no-one to care about their problems. People need people, and if you join a group or class of any kind you are pretty sure to meet someone who is on your wavelength and needs your friendship as much as you need hers. Fate may have been unkind to you, but try not to spoil these precious years with self-pity or resentment. Write down the things you really want from life, decide which are possible and start this very day to work towards the one you want the most. If you have a job, try to take a new pride in it; think out ways to do it better and enjoy it more. Does your work involve talking to people? Then if you've been rather reserved, why not

63

make a determined effort to be more positive? You never know what secret misery a person is suffering (as you may be yourself), and we all understand what a difference a smile and a pleasant word can make.

Did you know, by the way, that the very act of smiling does you good? In one of her delightful perceptive articles in *The Observer*, Katharine Whitehorn wrote:

> Science has come up with confirmation for my view that smiling, even if you don't feel like it, is more likely to cheer you up than glooming around with a long face. A smile is not, it seems, just a slit in the face. Smiling actually has a physiological point. You may not think of your face as simply a reservoir of blood for your brain, but apparently it is, and the 80 or so muscles that move it around are controlling the flow. The very act of smiling may regulate the flow to produce more 'happy' chemicals.

It may be a cliché, but I make no apology for suggesting that you count your blessings. Be grateful that you have a smooth unwrinkled face, that you can see and hear and run up and down stairs and plan for your future. You have many years ahead in which to fulfil your ambitions. Smaller blessings can be comforting, too, such as a good book, a cat on your lap or a friend you can telephone. And surely the great big blessing, in the prime of life, is just that you are *young*!

Middle age

On my fiftieth birthday somebody sent me a card with the following text: 'Age is largely a matter of mind; if you don't mind it doesn't matter.' How true!

Most of us feel with advancing years that it *doesn't* matter quite so much what people think of us. We're more settled in our ways, and we've come to the conclusion that we can't please everyone and it's no use trying. If you are rather diffident you might not see it quite like that, but I'm sure it's a sensible attitude.

Maturity helps to reduce shyness, but certain areas will probably remain that can only be dispelled by careful consideration and perseverance. Thought and effort can bring about remarkable improvements; the danger is just to let the years go by and do nothing about it. Perhaps the greatest hazard is anxiety, and this can take a heavy toll on the nervous system and drain our energy, quite apart from destroying our happiness. Deep relaxation, seriously studied and practised regularly, can help enormously. There are some excellent tape recordings on the market (see Appendix) and you can't do better than devote half an hour a day to the comforting and curative suggestions of the therapist.

Other problems for the middle-aged woman, whether she is shy or not, are the menopause and the loss of her youthful looks. You may know the delightful prayer: 'Give me the grace to accept what cannot be changed, the courage to change what can be changed, and the wisdom to know the difference'. The process of ageing certainly can't be changed, but we can change our attitude to one of cheerful acceptance rather than bitterness or despair.

As for the menopause there are, of course, various drugs available that may reduce unpleasant symptoms. On the other hand, they sometimes have side-effects and personally I'd avoid them as far as possible. Herbal remedies are safe and effective (and I'm a great believer in homeopathy) but we must never underestimate the natural power of the body to restore us to health *if we allow it to do so*. Nature can't possibly do its work efficiently if we are blocking the pipelines, as it were, with negative and anxious thoughts; a calm and relaxed attitude of mind is particularly important in middle life for the sake of our health, our looks and our happiness. I think the best approach during the menopause is to tell yourself that it will pass, just as those horrendous hot flushes pass if we do our best to ignore them. A friend of mine puts a little printed sticker on her envelopes: '*Grin and ignore it!*'. I think that's delightful.

None of us likes to grow old but if we fib about our age we shall feel much more self-conscious about it, worrying in case our secret is discovered. Somebody gave me that excellent advice long ago and I'm glad I took it; I have never pretended to be younger than I am and it's so much more relaxing just to be easy and honest about it. On the other hand, we ought never to say 'When you get to *my* age. . .'.

It is, of course, a natural temptation for a woman who doesn't look her age to lie about it, especially if she falls in love with a much younger man, but I've seen such heartbreak resulting from this kind of deception that I would always advise against it.

Nora, at fifty-five, looked at least ten years younger. She met and married Charles who was forty-four, letting him believe she was the same age. By the time she was sixty she really looked it and, in addition, she was terrified in case he saw the pension forms and suchlike, which arrived by post. Her secret was discovered when she bumped into an old schoolfriend who, in front of Charles, began to chatter gaily about their escapades of fifty years ago. Charles was appalled, not so much by her age as by her deception. They are still together, but if he had been less tolerant it might have been the end of their marriage.

Clothes can be a problem in middle age. Some women are so afraid of appearing like 'mutton dressed as lamb' that they choose outfits designed for 'the mature woman', which can be dull and ageing. There is a vast choice of charming clothes suitable for any age over thirty and these are the ones I'd recommend. We must, of course, wear what feels right and comfortable, but a few experiments along more youthful lines can produce some pleasant surprises.

A friend of mine in her fifties who usually wore drab tweeds was given a bright flowered skirt by her daughter. At first she was horrified and said she could never wear it, but she was finally persuaded to give it a try and now she realizes how flattering and graceful it looks. She has even bought herself another one in different colours, with a flowing scarf to match. A more adventurous approach to choosing clothes can do a lot for your self-image. If you feel unsure of yourself, take an imaginative friend along with you, someone who will give you an honest opinion but encourage you to be a little more dashing. The same applies to hair and make-up. There's nothing like a new hairstyle, or even a different colour of lipstick, to give us a boost, even though we may feel a little diffident at first.

There is probably no quality more essential to a happy middle age than cheerfulness. It's good for our looks, our health, our families, our friendships and our work. It isn't easy, when we feel the aches and pains of advancing years and when countless other problems conspire to make us fearful and unhappy, but the effort to be more positive and avoid self-pity will reward us beyond measure.

The later years

This is my own territory, so I feel very much at home on this page. You might think that a woman who has been shy all her life won't be likely to change after sixty, but I've known many who did, branching out after retirement into fresh fields of activity. Even a woman whose health has deteriorated in later life may find that her very infirmities lead to unexpected bonuses.

A widow called Mrs Miller went into hospital at seventy for a hip replacement. In the next bed, for the same operation, was Miss Lorrimer, aged sixty-three, who had been a handicrafts teacher until she retired. Mrs Miller used to be shy and at first she did not respond very kindly to her neighbour's friendly overtures. However, Miss Lorrimer was undeterred, and now they share a flat with another elderly woman and run a very successful soft-toy-making business. When Mrs Miller went into hospital she was lonely and frightened and dreading the future. Now, thanks to her own efforts, she is happy and fulfilled. She was, of course, very lucky to meet Miss Lorrimer but she was also wise enough to overcome her reticence and take advantage of her good fortune.

Let's consider some of the problems of old age and see how they may be overcome, or at least partially overcome.

One of the most worthwhile decisions we can make is to say goodbye to old quarrels and resentments. Nothing is worse for our health and peace of mind than bearing grudges, so if it is in your power to turn a difficult relationship into a more comfortable one, why not do it without delay? If you have behaved badly, apologize and ask for forgiveness. I've seen people suddenly look years younger when they have found the strength to make a gesture of this kind. It has a cleansing effect on the whole nervous system; all manner of aches and pains, caused by guilt and resentment, can vanish like magic. This is good advice for any age-group but as we grow older it is surely madness to allow the years ahead to be tarnished by needless acrimony. 'All you need is love' sang the Beatles, echoing the wisdom of St Paul: 'And now abideth faith, hope, charity, these three; but the greatest of these is charity'. (1 Corinthians 13:13.)

Some elderly people are very shy or even frightened of the young. They feel in some way ashamed of being old and infirm, imagining – often quite wrongly – that youngsters are making fun of them. Remember that many young people have grandparents whom they love very dearly and, in most cases, there is a special bond between young and old. If you are subjected to unkindness by a teenager, remind yourself that they will one day be old themselves (if they are lucky!) and then they will understand how hurtful a young person's intolerance can be. But try not to hold it against the whole mass of under-twenties who, for the most part, are much more caring than they are given credit for.

Many women are shy about being deaf, especially if they feel they have to keep their affliction secret. They miss people's remarks, pretend they heard when they didn't, make the wrong replies and get themselves into a muddle of misery. The best way out of all that is simply to be honest. Say you are hard of hearing (without apologizing for it), sit near the person who is speaking if you can, and *wear a hearing aid whenever necessary*. They are now so well designed as to be hardly visible. Persevere with those irritating whistles until you have mastered the device and know how to make modern technology work in your favour. If you find it impossible, ask for professional advice; hearing aids are available to suit almost every requirement and, although they can sometimes be quite costly, I've never met anyone who didn't consider the expenditure well worth the benefits.

We really shouldn't be shy about the normal failings that come to us in later life. Deficient hearing, eyesight and mobility are quite normal for the elderly and, unless we draw attention to them by too much comment or apology, are easily accepted by others. Many elderly people make so much fuss about their specs and sticks and pills and hearing aids that people are apt to smile or show irritation. Train yourself to make no comment when, for instance, you have to put on glasses for reading. It's such a temptation to invite interest and sympathy by saying 'Oh dear, I must put my specs on' and proceed to make a big song and dance about it. This is bound to be tedious for our companions and, consciously or subconsciously, we know very well that it is. You'll feel much more self-assured if you simply find your specs and put them on without comment. I know, because I went through it all myself when I first needed reading glasses. One day, an honest friend told me to put them on and shut up about it. I took her excellent advice and now I pass it on to you.

You'll be surprised how much calmer and more self-confident you feel if you can avoid referring to your problems, whether large or small, unless you have reason to do so. The pains of rheumatism, for instance, are hard to endure without complaint but 'grin and ignore it' is especially valuable advice to the elderly, even though it is so hard to follow. If you already work along these lines you will know just *how* valuable. Your friends will respect you for it and, better still, you will respect yourself – a very important aspect of confidence.

Our friends are of great value to us in later life, especially when we are housebound. We all need to communicate and this is where a cat, dog or budgie can make all the difference to an old person's well-being. You can talk to an animal without any shyness or anxiety; you can moan as much as you like about your aching limbs or your lost glasses or somebody you hate on television, and the only response will be a chirp from the cage or a placid feline gaze from the hearthrug. Human companions are also essential and if we can maintain a cheerful outlook, as I said in an earlier chapter, our friends will enjoy our company and we shall be far less lonely.

A positive and tolerant attitude of mind is of vital importance to anyone in a residential home. Most people are very sad to leave their own homes, and many find it hard to adjust to communal living when they have never been used to it, but those who can master their shyness and make an effort to be friendly are far more likely to settle down contentedly.

Growing older is hard to cope with but, as with all difficult situations, we can only make the best of what's available, both for ourselves and for others. Life is for living, at every age, and whether you're eighteen or eighty, the rest of your life begins today!

9

The Question of Guilt

Guilt, we all know, is a painfully destructive emotion and without it we should be a great deal happier and more confident. It is one of the main causes of shyness.

However, if we never felt guilty at all, whatever we did, there would certainly be something wrong with us; it can prompt us to apologize and mend our ways if we have behaved badly. Unfortunately, many people have a deep-seated sense of guilt that continually torments them and causes a lowering of self-esteem. Sometimes they don't quite know what ails them; all they know is that they seem to be stuck with this feeling and it makes them reserved and secretive, as well as unhappy.

We can think of guilt as coming under two headings: *needless* and *justifiable*.

Needless guilt

Let's consider why we suffer in this way and what we can do about it. By far the most common causes date back to childhood. If one (or both) of our parents continually found fault with us, refused to listen when we tried to explain our feelings, never praised us as other children were praised, humiliated us in front of friends or physically chastised us, it isn't surprising that we grew up feeling unworthy. This kind of treatment, sometimes amounting to cruelty, probably provoked some kind of retaliation on our part. This could give rise to a sense of shame, even though our reactions were quite understandable.

A victim of rape or any kind of sexual abuse may feel guilty, though heaven knows why unless she led the man on. If she is ill-treated or deserted by her husband, through no fault of her own, she may blame herself and feel degraded and unworthy of respect. The same thing can happen if a woman is rejected by one of her children, however little she may have deserved it. A friend's neglect can have the same effect, although the friend may in fact be the guilty one.

Needless guilt must be eradicated if we are to feel self-assured and comfortable with the people we meet. In Chapter 10 I shall discuss how deep relaxation, hypnotherapy and thought control can work a near-miracle in this respect.

I know a delightful woman called Susan who was consumed with guilt because her elderly widowed father died of a heart attack while she was on a motoring holiday in Italy with her husband. 'I should never have gone away and left him,' she wailed.

I couldn't agree. He was only seventy-six, he wasn't ill when they began their trip and was living contentedly in his little flat. 'Are you saying that you should have stopped taking holidays abroad for the rest of his life?' I asked her. 'He might have lived to be ninety. And think how unfair it would have been to your husband as well as to yourself.'

She took my point and felt better; her husband had been telling her the same thing. How could she have known that her father would die suddenly while she was away? If he had been ill before she left it would have been a different matter.

However, even in that case we would need to know the whole story (as always) before making a judgement. If her father were likely to be ill for years and was in good care, who could say that Susan should forgo a holiday abroad? Again, one must consider her husband's side of it. And what about the father himself? A generous and loving man might well have wanted them to go off and enjoy themselves. A compromise would be the answer, perhaps; certainly a holiday in a hotel so that she could be easily recalled in an emergency. And there is always the question of her relationship with her father. If he had been a selfish and unpleasant man, this would naturally have affected her behaviour!

I had an experience recently that caused me a few days of needless guilt. I was driving home one afternoon when a cat ran out in front of my car. It was killed outright, and although I was in no way to blame (it flashed out of a garden at the roadside, straight under my wheels), I'll never forget the distress of its elderly owners. The woman said they always knew it would happen one day, he was always running out like that and they shouldn't have had a cat when they lived on a main road. I'm a passionate cat-lover and I do wish he hadn't chosen my car for his demise.

Here we have examples of needless and of justifiable guilt: my own was needless, whereas theirs was understandable. If I'd been drinking, or driving too fast, I would have felt a justifiable guilt, wondering if otherwise I might have stopped in time.

Let's consider some more examples of needless guilt to comfort you if you've been suffering in this way. Rita is in her forties and lives in a suburban bungalow. She told me that she feels terribly guilty if the rooms get dusty or if a few weeds grow in the herbaceous border. She lives alone, so it isn't as if she were being pressured by an over-fussy partner. No, she has set her standards far too high and feels guilty if she fails to maintain them. I visited her once when she was getting over flu, and even then she couldn't stop apologizing for the fact that the windows needed cleaning! Such things don't bother me (and she knew that very well), but she couldn't stop talking about it.

Too much concern over household cleanliness is often a problem for women who lack confidence. I think they may be trying to compensate for some kind of lack or frustration in their lives. If you are in any way like Rita, try to discover the cause of your problem and make an effort to be less of a perfectionist; you'll feel a lot more relaxed and self-assured if you can manage it.

— Joyce feels guilty because she thinks she didn't do enough for her mother who died recently in a residential home. 'I should have had her to live with us,' she says. 'She *wanted* to come and live with us – she was always on about it.'

'What about Bill?' I asked her. 'He wouldn't have liked that, would he?'

She confessed that her husband dreaded the thought of her mother moving into their small semi. I could understand it: I knew Joyce's mother. She never stopped talking and everything she said was not only negative and disruptive but delivered at a high level of decibels. It's a wonder the staff at the residential home didn't leave!

So Joyce has no need to feel guilty. She would have felt much guiltier if she had given in to her mother and wrecked her marriage. Bill is a reasonable and pleasant man and she loves him dearly. All this guilt of hers is making him very unhappy, and she really ought to cast it off and concentrate on being a cheerful and sensible wife. We often feel guilty when someone close to us dies, wondering if we did all we reasonably could to make them happy, but we must live in the present, not in the past, and try to cast aside any useless regrets.

So much for needless guilt. I'm sure you can think of many examples, either in your own life or in the lives of your friends. If you feel you are suffering in this way, look at the causes as objectively as you can and do all in your power to free yourself through hypnotherapy, meditation, prayer or whatever you feel is right for you.

Justifiable guilt

Let us face up, first of all, to the problem of someone who has committed a grave offence. If we have injured someone and there is no way of making amends, it won't be easy to eradicate a very understandable – and indeed necessary – sense of shame. Decent and caring people do, of course, feel guilty; it's the natural consequence of wrong-doing. Nevertheless, if we are continually tortured by it, long after the event, no good can come of it and we must do all we can to put it behind us. In the first instance a sense of guilt will lead us to put things right as far as possible but, unless we control it, it can undermine the courage and optimism we need to make the best of the situation for ourselves and others. Guilt and shame are both destructive emotions, and shame is particularly difficult to cope with when we feel it on account of the bad conduct of someone close to us, rather than ourselves.

Remorse is different. A genuine sense of contrition is a good and compassionate feeling, concerned not so much with ourselves as with the person we have wronged. However, to be consumed with remorse is to live in the past, and we need to think positively about the future if we are to achieve that inner peace and stability we are looking for.

Guilt is, by its very nature, obsessive. Round and round it goes, like an endless tape recording, poisoning the system, eating away at our happiness and our self-esteem, blocking our progress in whatever creative direction we want to be travelling. Tell yourself that it's got to stop and that it's jolly well *going* to stop. Put on another 'tape' at the very first sign of these obsessive guilty thoughts. Press a mental button that instantly switches off the dreaded sequence and replaces it with a programme of your own choosing, positive and pleasurable. Easier said than done, you may say, and it certainly requires determination and perseverance if the Substitution Technique is new to you (see page 88). Nevertheless, thousands of students will testify to their success with this method, which has been advocated by psychologists for many years and is more widely practised today than ever before.

What can be done? First of all, as with the smallest of our misdemeanours, do whatever is possible to put the matter right. Express your genuine sorrow and if you understand the reasons for your behaviour, explain them. Perhaps you'd had a drink too many; this can make us speak our minds too freely, as many of us know to our cost – myself included. Perhaps you were suffering from depression? Or provoked to an unendurable degree? A build-up of resentment over the years may suddenly have exploded as a result of some seemingly trivial incident, catching you unawares. There is usually some relevant factor that should be taken into account by you yourself, even if the injured party is not interested in hearing about it.

We may feel guilty on account of something we *haven't* done, either through procrastination or through lack of courage. It may be any one of a thousand things, large or small – an apology owed, or money, or an invitation – but the longer we leave it, the worse we feel. So why not take action at once if there is something of this nature on your mind?

Secrets

Most of us have some aspect of our lives we would prefer no-one to know about, something we are ashamed of. This is not unusual; we'd probably be amazed if we knew how many such secrets are hidden away in the guilty consciences of our friends and relations. If you have such a secret, make a firm resolution not to repeat the misdemeanour and then try to forget it. There are endless causes for guilt and we have all sinned at some time or other, in big ways or small. We must make amends as far as possible and then forgive ourselves, just as we forgive others. Of course we are bound to feel guilty if we continue to offend. The matter is in our own hands. The best cure for shyness is to *like* oneself. I have learnt from my own experience that if I behave badly my self-esteem goes down and, with it, my self-assurance. When we are feeling guilty it can be a great relief to confess our errors to a trusted friend, someone who will listen uncritically, understand us, comfort us, and never betray our confidences. Such friends are a gift from heaven and we should be eternally grateful for them.

Guilt on a small scale

The guilt we feel about small errors is often out of all proportion to its cause. Some people can't make a mistake of any kind without being overwhelmed by guilt. But *everyone* makes mistakes, and we really shouldn't take them too seriously. We may do in a day a dozen or more little things we wish we hadn't, from losing our temper to forgetting to post a letter, but the only course, having done all we can to put the matter right, is to *forget about it*. Thinking about an unhappy occasion, whether serious or trivial, only perpetuates our distress; it's like a mosquito bite – it won't stop itching until we leave it alone!

We all know the misery of sleepless nights spent going over

76

what we said and what the other person said, and what they meant, and what they might have thought we meant . . . and oh, if we could only take it all back and start again! It's a sinking ship, isn't it? It doesn't do anything for you, except perhaps to give you a headache or indigestion. The way I deal with such eventualities and get a good night's sleep, is to practise deep relaxation and thought control. You may already be doing something similar, but if not you'll find instructions in the next chapter. I think it's the most important chapter in the book; that's why I saved it until last.

Making those we love feel guilty is sure to upset us, so we should avoid it as far as possible, although this doesn't mean we can't be honest with them if we feel they have behaved badly. Conversely, don't allow others to make *you* feel guilty. We must be constantly on guard against this because, unfortunately, there is often someone around who will try! Never, *never* bear grudges; people who do so lose respect for themselves. If you think you might be guilty of this, consider honestly how you can be rid of it. It will harm you much more than the recipient.

Indecision causes guilt and can also lead to depression. If we lack confidence we are inclined to avoid making any decision at all, in case it's the wrong one. Cultivate a more adventurous approach. After taking careful stock of the situation, possibly writing down the pros and cons, make your decision without more ado. But always be flexible. Be prepared to change your plans if some unexpected new factor emerges.

Another enemy is procrastination. 'Do it *now*!' is my motto; otherwise I find that a list of things to be done builds up in my subconscious mind and causes needless anxiety. Why not consider what you might do today to shorten your list of outstanding jobs? You'll be pleased with yourself if you make a start on them, and a feeling of inner contentment is a major goal if we are to be self-confident.

Sexual guilt

This is a problem that may need professional therapy. Women who feel that they are not providing satisfaction – or not achieving it for themselves – can suffer deeply on this account. An honest talk with one's partner is the best solution; men and women need to understand each other's sexual needs if they are to be happy and comfortable together, and any loving relationship can be improved by a good heart-to-heart.

If you are unable to reach orgasm, don't be tempted to fake it; you will worry in case he suspects! *Talk* about it, but be sure that you don't, however subtly, question his kindness or virility. Good sex depends on a warm and tender relationship; none of us feels warm and tender if we are being cricitized on such a delicate matter. For a happy love life, both men and women must be able to tell one another what pleases them, and if you are too reticent the years may go by with a build-up of frustration and guilt (possibly on both sides) and no improvement in the situation.

You will have noticed that all through this book I have constantly been advising honesty and truth in all problematic human relationships. Shyness is often the reason for dishonesty, but if you can manage to communicate your troubles, you will find a new sense of security. Success breeds success, and confidence breeds confidence.

Guilt about our sexual misdemeanours, such as infidelity, is quite another matter, and I wouldn't presume to offer advice in this area. We can only do what we feel is right in relation to all the factors concerned. A sense of guilt may be unavoidable; all we can do is to control it or to alter our conduct. And honesty may not always be the best policy!

Spoil yourself a little

Molly, who is in her fifties, cannot enjoy the smallest treat without feeling guilty. Even half an hour's relaxation, just for the pleasure of it, is taboo. She can never put her feet up with a magazine, sipping coffee or a glass of wine. And not only does she find it impossible to relax herself, but she can't let others relax either. I daren't tell her about my own little extravagances; she'd try to make me feel guilty about them!

I asked Molly if she had always felt like this and she said she couldn't remember a time when she hadn't. She had a very strict religious upbringing and her parents wouldn't allow her to go out and enjoy herself with other girls of her own age. She did a lot of good work for the church and married a young man in the choir who had a similar lifestyle to her own. She has now brought up her family and deserves a bit of fun, but fun is not a word in her vocabulary. She would feel guilty having fun, just as she feels guilty if she takes five minutes off from the housework to put her feet up. Her husband is rather a mean man, but she has a legacy of her own and could easily lash out a bit if she chose to.

If you are in any way like Molly, uneasy about your leisure, short on fun, try to accept the fact that we all need to spoil ourselves a little from time to time. Arrange an outing that is not for any purpose but your own delight. Buy yourself a little present. Get some luxurious bath essence and relax in a hot bath until your tensions melt away. Buy the latest issue of your favourite magazine and a box of chocolates. (If you're on a diet, to hell with it for once!) Tell yourself that you deserve a few treats and that no-one is going to do you out of them. And make a firm resolve, before you start, that *you won't feel guilty about it*!

10
The Need for Relaxation

You would never have read so far unless you really wanted to overcome your shyness. A deep desire for liberation is an essential part of the cure, and if you want it enough you will make the effort to bring about the changes you dream of. Relaxation will help this to happen.

Nervous tension causes unhappiness. It also causes headaches, indigestion and many other complaints. Deep relaxation brings a calm state of mind as well as a release from muscular tension. As a result you will experience a new sense of physical well-being, besides feeling more self-assured and more strongly in control of the life you wish to lead.

If you persevere, you can learn to relax at will. Think of a situation in which you habitually suffer from tension and lack of confidence. Now imagine how you would feel in the same situation if you had the ability, whenever you chose, to disperse any tension and enter into a comfortable state of inner relaxation. It may seem like an impossible dream but I can promise that it is perfectly feasible. Once you have learnt the technique you can relax your mind in a crowded train, a supermarket queue, at a party, or wherever you feel the need for it. No one will know you are doing it – except that they will see a calm and confident person instead of someone who is timid and uncertain.

You may be anxious in case you find yourself unable to reach this deep level of relaxation, but I have been assured by highly qualified practitioners that almost everyone can develop the skill, and that women seem to find it easier than men. For some people the improvement is immediate, for others more gradual, but if you devote yourself to it for fifteen minutes or so every morning and evening, you will be amazed by the results. You may suddenly find yourself speaking more freely in discussions with friends, making firmer decisions, taking the initiative on occasions when you used to hang back, and coping more easily with difficult personal relationships.

Dedication and perseverance are essential for success in any project – learning a language, driving a car, writing a book, making a garden. . . . Relaxation is, paradoxically, a skill that requires a steadfast and determined approach, with no opting out because we are too busy, too tired or too discouraged. The rewards are immensely worthwhile, whatever your problem, and for anyone who is shy there can be no better therapy.

How to relax

I sometimes give lectures and conduct weekend courses on a subject I call 'Creative Living'. This covers many approaches to a happier life, but especially the need for a relaxed state of mind. The method I use when people are new to the subject is to be found in books on various aspects of relaxation – Yoga, meditation, thought-control, self-hypnosis, etc. – and it entails sitting in a comfortable position, closing your eyes, breathing regularly and easily, letting all your muscles go limp and counting slowly backwards from 100 to 1. Because you are concentrating solely on the next number, you will find that intrusive thoughts are gradually excluded, although it may be some time before you are able to count all the way back to number 1. Some people go back to 100 when other thoughts arrive, but this is up to you. I just press on! When I first tried it I couldn't even get to 95 without thinking of something else! If you find it difficult to relax your muscles, start by 'dropping your shoulders' and then let your jaw muscles go. This will very often help to get your whole body relaxed.

People sometimes suggest that we can relax by flopping in a chair and making our minds a blank. I don't think this is possible; the conscious mind is always occupied by some concept or other. We can, however, only embrace one notion at a time, and this is why we are able to calm the mind by concentrating entirely on numbers. You will find you can gradually count further and further without admitting extraneous thoughts, and a sensation of peace and tranquillity will replace any nervous tension that may have troubled you when you began.

This, of course, is an excellent way of getting to sleep, rather like counting sheep! Many of my students, even confirmed insomniacs, report that they drop off long before they get back to number 1, and wake up next morning surprised and delighted to find that they 'really did it!' Needless to say, it doesn't always work at once; it might take weeks or even months before you get the full benefit, but if you practise with faith and determination you will gain admission to a new world of self-assurance, knowing you can relax at will in difficult situations.

There are many other methods of inducing a relaxed state of mind. You may find it easier to count your breaths, to concentrate on some pleasant object in the room or repeat a chosen word or phrase (*mantra*). Meditation or prayer may be your chosen way. Everyone must find her individual approach. Some people prefer to count back from 10 to 1, and in this case it's best to go back to 10 if you get side-tracked. Some like to start at 300 and count back in threes (it certainly occupies the mind more fully!). But for those who are unfamiliar with these techniques, the 100–1 method is usually effective. If intrusive thoughts persist you should try to view them with detachment, as if they were of no concern to you; it's surprising how soon they disperse if you simply watch them go by and disregard them. 'How the blazes can I do that?' you may protest. 'I can *never* get my problems out of my mind!' That's what I used to think myself. Try it and you'll see how well it works.

The power of auto-suggestion

Having succeeded in counting back as far as number 1, without too many hold-ups, you will be feeling much calmer and quite sleepy. The next step is the most important of all: auto-suggestion. This is the way you begin to cure your shyness. When we are half-way between waking and sleeping, as we are in deep relaxation (known as the Alpha level), we can most easily make contact with the subconscious mind. In this way we are able to give ourselves positive suggestions to replace any negative conditioning from the past. (Remember those engrams!) This is why auto-suggestion can achieve successful results when other treatments have failed. And this is why it's so helpful to assess the reasons for our shyness, in order to remove the damaging influences that lurk in the depths of our minds. This is also why drugs can have no lasting benefit: they do nothing to reach the basic cause of the problem. At the end of this book you will find suggestions for further reading to help you to master these techniques.

Many years ago I knew a woman who couldn't pass her piano exams because she was so nervous. She could play the pieces perfectly at home, but in the examination room she was quite unable to perform. After several sessions with a qualified hypnotist, she learnt to practise self-hypnosis and soon passed her piano exams with flying colours. Not only that, but she also lost the desire to smoke, although she had not mentioned her addiction to the hypnotherapist. Such unexpected bonuses are apparently quite common.

When I told this friend that I was having trouble with hypertension, she urged me to try hypnosis. I was rather apprehensive, knowing little about it, but I was ready to try anything. Let me tell the rest of the story by quoting from an article I wrote for *Vogue* in 1978:

I had been suffering for many years from acute nervous tension, brought about, I think, by my highly-strung temperament combined with the ever-increasing conflict of trying to do two full-time jobs. To complicate matters, there were also some difficult personal relationships. This, of course, was a common situation and it seemed I should just have to live with it, taking the tranquillisers and sleeping pills my doctor prescribed. But the drugs made me drowsy and I needed a clear brain for my work. My anxiety increased. I suffered from every one of the following dismal complaints: headaches, fibrositis, backache, dizzy spells, indigestion, insomnia, catarrh, and fits of depression. A pathetic tale indeed! And the misery of guilt was added to my problems because I knew that my ailments were largely the results of my own state of mind.

A friend advised hypnosis. I had already studied Yoga and meditation – albeit half-heartedly – and I knew there was a lot to be said for the power of mind over matter, so I made an appointment with a qualified hypnotist. After only three visits I threw away my tranquillisers and sleeping pills. That was six years ago and I have never needed them since.

Well, it's now *sixteen* years ago, and the same applies! I never have headaches because I can relax them away at the first sign of tension. Most of my ailments have vanished but they sometimes reappear if I forget my relaxation sessions. It's rather like slimming: your whole lifestyle has to change if the results are to be permanent. A very comforting aspect of this kind of therapy is that there are no unpleasant side-effects, as there may be with tranquillisers.

Another extract from that article in *Vogue* will show you how self-hypnosis can be helpful in the most surprising ways.

I was writing a teenage novel with a hang gliding background and I knew I should have to make a flight myself before I could write a certain chapter with the proper authority. My son is an instructor so it was easy to arrange a tandem flight with him. It was not so easy to face the occasion with equanimity, as it entailed racing full-tilt to the edge of a 300-foot drop and launching myself into the void! My head for heights is not specially good, so this was obviously another occasion to benefit from self-hypnosis. Several weeks before the event, I began to give myself daily suggestions that I should be calm and confident and suffer no unpleasant apprehensions. It worked. I was never afraid, and the flight was one of the most glorious experiences of my life.

You may be wondering how it is possible to give yourself suggestions when you are under hypnosis. The reason is that you are by no means 'asleep' in the accepted sense of the word; you are acutely aware of everything that is taking place – more keenly aware, perhaps, than in the ordinary waking state – and when you transmit positive suggestions to your subconscious mind they will eventually be effective, provided you think about them deeply and do not allow other thoughts to intrude.

It is very important, if you consult a hypnotherapist, to be sure that he or she is fully qualified. The British Society of Medical and Dental Hypnosis will supply details of qualified practitioners in your area (their address is given on page 94), but you should first discuss the matter with your GP. Hypnosis is now so widely and successfully used in childbirth, dentistry, slimming, phobias, stammering, curing the smoking habit, etc. that most doctors are sympathetic. The hypnotist who treated me was also a GP. We all know about those appalling stage demonstrations which, quite naturally, scare the uninitiated, but a qualified hypnotherapist will utilize his powers in a purely beneficial way and you need have no fears whatsoever. The whole experience is comforting and enjoyable, as well as curative.

I expect you'd like to know what happens when you visit a hypnotist. The first thing is to have an informal chat about your problems. Then you will sit in a comfortable chair and prepare to relax your whole body, bit by bit, according to his instructions. (I say 'his', but of course there are many female practitioners.) There's no question of him gazing into your eyes and taking control of you; he will only help you to help yourself by inducing a very deep and special state of relaxation, both physical and mental. He will probably explain that relaxation produces calm, calm produces confidence and confidence produces self-control. This is fundamental to the therapy and it relates, of course, very closely to the needs of someone who is shy. When you are sufficiently relaxed he will give you a number of beneficial suggestions which will reach your subconscious mind and help to eradicate any painful hang-ups from the past.

This is the kind of thing he will say. 'You will become increasingly less anxious, less easily upset, more confident and relaxed in every way. You will be less easily fatigued, more positive in whatever you have to do. You will sleep more soundly, your memory will improve, and every day will bring a deepening sense of well-being. . .'. And so on, including references to your own particular problems.

You will also be taught how to reach a very deep state of relaxation on your own so that you have no need for frequent visits. The charge is usually about £25 for an hour's session, so it's prudent to become self-reliant as soon as possible! A number of excellent relaxation tapes are available (see Appendix) and if you listen daily you will notice the benefits very quickly.

Shyness, as we all know, is basically a state of mind, and the mind affects the whole nervous system. If you think you've lost your purse you break into a sweat, your pulse races, your knees tremble and you feel sick. When you find it again, with the money still inside, all the unpleasant symptoms disappear and you are back to normal. In fact you may be on cloud nine, smiling with relief and thankfulness.

You have probably been conditioning yourself for years to believe that you have lost your self-confidence – or even that you never had any! This negative conditioning may have been helped along by other people or circumstances that have lowered your morale. Perhaps you have searched everywhere, as you thought, for that 'purse' of confidence and when you failed to find it you felt even more demoralized. Had you known it, that precious purse was safely in your keeping – deep in your own being; you just didn't know where to look. This reminds me of the Buddhist legend about a prince who had everything except the Pearl of Wisdom. He searched the whole world in vain, until at last he realized he was wearing it on his own forehead!

You may have heard the maxim: 'Day by day, in every way, I'm getting better and better.' It has become a cliché and a bit of a joke, but Emile Coué originated the phrase to help thousands of patients to cure themselves of all manner of complaints by repeating these words twenty times every morning and evening. Ulcers, asthma, rheumatism, bronchitis, glaucoma, tuberculosis, paralysis and many types of neurosis seemed to vanish like magic. Doctors simply couldn't understand it. In his marvellous book *Self Mastery Through Conscious Auto-suggestion* he says:

> We possess within us a force of incalculable power, which, when we handle it unconsciously, is often prejudicial to us. If on the contrary we direct it in a conscious and wise manner, it gives us the mastery of ourselves, and allows us not only to escape and aid others to escape from physical and mental ills, but also to live in relative happiness, whatever the conditions in which we find ourselves.

The 'incalculable power', of course, is the power of auto-suggestion, which many people are in the habit of using negatively. 'I'm sure to make a mess of it,' they tell themselves and their friends when some examination is approaching. 'I'll be petrified if someone asks me a question.' 'I'm sure to get a headache when I go to see So-and-So.' 'I always feel terrible if I wake up in the night.' And so it goes on – negative conditioning, day after day – and every time we repeat these dreary forebodings we help to bring them about. Positive suggestions are equally effective, and if we bear this in mind, not only in conversations with other people but in our silent interior conversations with ourselves, the quality of our lives will be enormously enriched. It's especially important to apply an optimistic attitude to the practice of relaxation. Tell yourself that you can and will succeed, and that nothing is going to stop you. 'Conscious auto-suggestion, made with confidence, with faith, with perseverance, realises itself mathematically, within reason,' said Emile Coué. (He added 'within reason', of course, to avoid disappointing people who might expect the impossible!)

If we persist with pessimistic talk we do more damage than we realize, both to ourselves and to other people. On the other hand positive comment brings confidence and good cheer. Auto-suggestion is so powerful that it can bring us either misery and ill-health or countless blessings; it depends entirely on how we use it.

The Substitution Technique

This is concerned with thought-control, which is surely essential to our well-being. Without it we can so easily be sucked into a downward spiral of depression, one anxious thought giving rise to another. In his book *'Thought-control in Everyday Life'*, James Alexander writes:

> One thought can only be driven out of the mind by another thought. This is done by substitution. You can pass from one thought to the other very rapidly, but you cannot think of both at the same time . . . when disturbing thoughts enter the mind switch them aside instantly.

We all know how dangerous it can be to allow our negative thinking to get out of hand. Guilt, self-consciousness and anxiety can build up into a veritable maelstrom of nervous tension if we do not understand how to control them.

Because we can only think of one thing at a time, we have the power to free ourselves from the tyranny of painful speculations by replacing them with positive and constructive ones. However, *it must be done at once*. If we allow our negative thoughts the slightest leeway they will take command. We can only banish them by putting new and beneficial ideas in their place. This is sometimes known as the Substitution Technique, and in order to practise it successfully you need to do a little planning in advance. Unpleasant thoughts can attack us without warning, triggered by a chance remark, a television programme, a newspaper report or some wild and unheralded horror from the subconscious mind – a memory or even a dream. On these occasions we need to be ready with a substitute; it's no good thinking: 'Oh, my God, what can I think about that's nice?' Nothing suitable is likely to come to mind! What you need, therefore, is a storehouse of positive ideas, specially prepared for those difficult moments.

A favourite substitution of my own is the face of a beloved cat, the feel of her fur and the sound of her purring. Three senses are involved and when I replace a troubling thought with this (for me) utterly delightful concept, I am free at once from the threat of nervous tension or dejection. Images of nature – creatures, flowers and landscapes – serve very well, but you could think of a certain picture, a line of verse or a quotation from the Bible. Anything will suffice so long as it gives you pleasure and comfort and has no painful associations.

It is obviously necessary, from time to time, to consider unpleasant matters in order to decide what is to be done about them; I'm certainly not advising you to 'put your head in the sand' or 'live in a dream world'. We have the choice, however, of dealing with problems cheerfully and constructively or letting them drag us down. We must do all we can to combat that 'downward spiral of depression' which is such a threat to our well-being. If you practise substitution correctly you will experience an ascending spiral of improvement, taking you day by day from shyness to self-assurance. This is no pipe-dream: it's a realistic promise.

I warmly recommend to you a book on this subject called *The Silva Mind Control Method* by José Silva and Philip Miele (Souvenir Press). This book describes how to control your thoughts by creating a mental screen on which you picture specific benefits you wish to receive. The method entails thinking very briefly of the condition you wish to remedy and then moving the desired picture in from the left to replace the unwanted image (the left signifies the future, the right the past). For example, if you can't get to sleep, picture yourself for a moment lying awake, and then immediately substitute a mental image of yourself fast asleep, comfortable and contented. This method works very well for anyone who is shy. Picture the timid person you may be just now, and replace it with the woman you want to be – relaxed and sure of herself, doing whatever she has to do with easy confidence.

José Silva has this to say:

Among the laws of the universe there seems to be a sort of cosmic Bill of Rights which guarantees that all of us, no matter how high or low, no matter how bright or dull, can take part in causing lawful things to happen through the firmness of our desire, belief and expectancy. This was said earlier, and better, almost 2,000 years ago, as reported by Mark in the New Testament: 'What things soever ye desire, when ye pray, believe that ye receive them, and ye shall receive them.'

Picture yourself as you want to be

I have been using many practical methods over the years to gain more confidence, but none is more effective or astounding than picturing myself as I want to be. It's similar to the Substitution Technique but it can be used to prepare oneself in advance for future occasions that are likely to prove troublesome. I do quite a lot of lecturing and the prospect of addressing a large and knowledgeable audience can seem very daunting. The secret is to relax very deeply – down to the Alpha level – and then to imagine myself stepping up onto the platform feeling calm and happy and self-assured. It always works. If I have to make a difficult telephone call I see myself picking up the phone, feeling totally relaxed and expressing myself clearly and pleasantly, refusing to be upset by any unforeseen (or foreseen!) comments from the other end. If I am going to a party (and I'm still inclined to feel shy at parties), I picture myself looking good, feeling good and thoroughly enjoying myself. A visit to the dentist can be prepared for in just the same way: no apprehension or anxiety. The power of auto-suggestion works like a miracle, except that it isn't a miracle at all! It's simply the laws of nature fulfilling themselves normally because they are not being blocked. It's just like mathematics. The principle is infallible and when we get our sums wrong it's because we haven't implemented it properly. Sometimes I forget that I've pictured myself feeling relaxed and happy in a difficult situation, and when the time arrives I'm quite surprised to feel so calm. Then I remember: 'Of *course* – I programmed myself!' It works with the precision of the computer; feed in the positive suggestions and you can't go wrong. It's only when the computer goes wrong that problems arise!

When you have practised this method successfully a few times, your faith in its working will be established and you will gain more confidence. If you don't *expect* to succeed, your doubts can get in the way, although I know of many cases where people have achieved great things in spite of some early scepticism. We only need to see these laws at work in our everyday lives to lose our doubts and to make every effort to utilize the marvellous powers we have all been given. Not to use them, as I said in my introduction, is to starve in the midst of plenty.

The beauty of meditation

In his excellent book *Teach Yourself Meditation*, James Hewitt, who also writes on Yoga, explains how the practice of meditation will 'help you to maintain physical health and mental clarity and equanimity'. Like self-hypnosis, it produces a calming of the nervous system which not only relieves mental and muscular tension but can also reduce high blood pressure and many other symptoms of stress. Transcendental Meditation, far from being an 'airy-fairy', mystical practice, is taught at the U.S. Army War College to help soldiers to adjust to stress, and many American universities, including Yale, offer degree courses in the subject.

Yoga is perhaps the most widely practised of all the relaxing arts, and classes are available in many areas. If you find the physical exercises difficult, you can still derive great benefit from the meditative aspects. It seems to me that the different names we use for these practices – meditation, self-hypnosis, auto-suggestion, thought-control – are apt to disguise the fact that they all work in very much the same way: relaxing our muscles and our minds, and creating the conditions in which we can be in tune with nature and function at peak efficiency. If you are a believer you will probably think of this as being in harmony with God.

Good health is our natural state. Children and animals are seldom sick unless they meet with an accident, catch an infection or come under the negative influence of someone else. Sickness is very largely brought about by fear and worry, by anger and frustration, by resentment, guilt, greed and envy. When we reach a deep state of relaxation, as in meditation, these negative emotions simply melt away, leaving us free to build within ourselves the kind of person we really want to be.

Peace of mind and self-assurance

There's something about those words that makes me feel calm and happy. I wonder if they have the same effect on you? The very sounds of the syllables have a ring of tranquillity, as if they were finding an echo somewhere deep within me.

I hope you will follow straight through from the last page of this book to the first page of a new life, working steadily forward to overcome your shyness and establish a new pattern of confident living. If you do, you will relate more easily to other people, attempt all kinds of activities you used to avoid and embrace a wider and more rewarding field of experience.

To sum up, this is the programme I suggest:

1. Practise deep relaxation for fifteen minutes every morning and evening.

2. During that time, give yourself positive suggestions related to overcoming your shyness.

3. Practise the Substitution Technique whenever painful thoughts disturb your equanimity.

4. Use your imagination to picture yourself as you want to be, knowing that with faith and perseverance (provided you are not picturing the impossible), that image will be realized.

I leave you with my favourite quotation from Emile Coué: *'We are what we make of ourselves and not what circumstances make us.'*

Further Reading

Berne, Eric *Games People Play* (Penguin, 1970).

Coleman, Vernon *How to Stop Feeling Guilty* (Sheldon Press, 1986).

Coué, Emile *Self Mastery Through Conscious Auto-suggestion* (Unwin Hyman).

Dickson, Anne *A Woman in Your Own Right* (Quartet, 1982).

Gibran, Kahlil *The Prophet* (Pan Books, 1980).

Harris, Thomas *I'm OK – You're OK* (Pan Books, 1973).

Hauck, Paul *Calm Down* (Sheldon Press, 1980).

Hewitt, James *Teach Yourself Meditation* (Hodder and Stoughton, 1984).

Hewitt, James *Yoga and You* (Tandem Books).

Honey, Peter *Solving Your Personal Problems* (Sheldon Press, 1983).

Horwood, Janet *Comfort for Depression* (Sheldon Press, 1988).

Maltz, Maxwell *Psycho-Cybernetics* (Wilshire Book Co. (USA), 1967).

Markham, Ursula *Hypnothink* (Thorson Publishing Group, 1985).

Peale, Norman Vincent *A Guide to Confident Living* (World's Work Ltd (USA), 1955).

Peale, Norman Vincent *The Power of Positive Thinking* (World's Work Ltd (USA)).

Silva, José and Miele, Peter *The Silva Mind Control Method* (Souvenir Press).

Tavris, Carol (Ed.) *Every Woman's Emotional Well-being* (Doubleday (USA)).

Trine, Ralph Waldo *In Tune with the Infinite* (Bell).

Watts, Alan W. *The Wisdom of Insecurity* (Rider).

Waxman, David *Hypnosis* (Unwin Paperbacks, 1984).

Useful Addresses

Association for Stammerers
c/o The Finsbury Centre
Pine Street
London EC1R 5LH

British Society of Medical and Dental Hypnotists
42 Links Road
Ashstead
Surrey KT21 2HJ

Brook Advisory Centres
153a East Street
London SE17 2SD
01-708 1234
(Or see your phone book for local centre)
Advice about birth control for young people

Citizens' Advice Bureau
See your local phone book

Gingerbread
Advice and help for lone parents and their children
35 Wellington Street
London WC2E 7BN
01-240 0953

Incest Crisis Line
Open 24 hours a day for anyone who is being, or has been,
abused.
32 Newbury Close
Northolt
Middlesex UB5 4JF
01-422 5100/890 4732

Lifeline
(Battered Wives)
PO Box 251
Marlborough
Wiltshire

National Federation of 18+ Groups
Nicholson House
Old Court Road
Newent
Gloucester
0531 821 210

Organisation for Parents Under Stress
106 Godstone Road
Whyteleafe
Surrey CR3 O6B

Relate
(Formerly the National Marriage Guidance Council)
Herbert Gray College
Little Church Street
Rugby CV21 3AP
0788 73241

Relaxation for Living
29 Burwood Park Road
Walton-on-Thames
Surrey KT12 5LH

Samaritans
See your local phone book, or phone 01-626 9000

Young People's Counselling Service
Free, confidential counselling for anyone aged between 16 and 30
Tavistock Centre
120 Belsize Lane
London NW3 5BA
01-435 7111 ext 337

Relaxation Tapes

Institute of Tape Learning
P.O. Box 4
Hemel Hempstead
Herts

The Matthew Manning Centre
39 Abbeygate Street
Bury St Edmunds
Suffolk IP33 1LW

People Products Ltd
141 Albany Road
Earlsdon
Coventry CV5 6ND

Overcoming Common Problems

A successful and popular series to give you practical help for the emotional and medical problems of everyday life.

Paperbacks £1·95 to £4·95
Available from all good bookshops

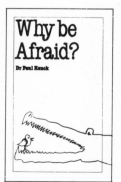